ANDREW!

SAVAGERY FROM THE SEA

WTVJ-CH. 4

August 24, 1992

BY THE STAFF OF THE

Sun-Sentinel

FORT LAUDERDALE, FLORIDA

TRIBUNE
PUBLISHING

ORLANDO, FLORIDA
1992

This book was made possible by the extraordinary day-to-day coverage of Hurricane Andrew by the reporters, photographers, editors, artists, editorial assistants and researchers of the Sun-Sentinel, Fort Lauderdale, Fla.

ANDREW!
SAVAGERY FROM THE SEA

Editor
John Christie

Associate editor/stories
John deGroot

Associate editor/photographs
Jerry Lower

Designer
Greg Carannante

Chief copy editor
Mindy Brown

Informational graphics editor
Scott Anderson

Page designers
Chip Halvorsen, Heather M. Lajewski, Dean Lockwood, Scott Nystrom,
Bill Henderson (Tribune Publishing), Robb Montgomery (*XS*)

Research
Renee Anise, Debby Bradford, Dottie Horrocks, Bob Isaacs,
MaryAnn McCarthy, Jackie McGrath, R.J. Petrovich

Color technology
Karin Devendorf, Robert Dunn, John Herbst, Glenn Kirchhoff, Deborah LaFogg, Michael
Matute, Gregg Olshove, Lyn Rex, Kathryn Romeu-Harrison, Darryl Tait

Sun-Sentinel
Publisher and president: Thomas P. O'Donnell
Editor: Gene Cryer
Managing editor: Earl Maucker

For information about this and other books from Tribune Publishing, contact:
Tribune Publishing
P.O. Box 1100
Orlando, Fla. 32802-1100
(407) 420-5680

ISBN 0-941263-71-1

Cover photo
A south Dade County, Fla., neighborhood devastated by Hurricane Andrew.
By Carl Seibert
Contents page photo
Lucy Cadavid with daughter Evelyn in their West Kendall home where the family rode out the storm.
By John Curry

CONTENTS

HURRICANE ANDREW

Out of the Whirlwind

Then the Lord answered Job out of the whirlwind: "Where were you when I laid the foundations of the earth? Tell me if you have understanding."
— Job 38: 1,4

The young man stares at broken trees, roofless stores and streets littered with signs — the transformed landmarks of a once-tidy, suburban South Florida town.

He is a soldier, one of thousands sent here to help clear away the destruction from Hurricane Andrew, the storm called our most destructive national disaster.

He turns away from the alien landscape, overwhelmed.

The soldier bends down and picks up a handful of leaves.

"It's little by little," says Timothy Skeen, 19, a private first class with the 82nd Airborne Division. "At first, we started moving trees, and moving trees and all kinds of debris and it just never stops. But once you finish a little area, you can see it is a little

CRUMBLED LIVES
A man searches for what can be salvaged from the rubble that was once his mobile home near Tamiami Airport in south Dade County.

CARL SEIBERT

better."

Pfc. Skeen is part of a unit of men in burgundy berets based at a SunBank in Cutler Ridge. The soldiers haul wind-scattered debris in a trash bin-turned-wheelbarrow. They camp in the bank's drive-through lanes. Trying to make things a little better.

The concept seems out of place in such vast destruction. As out of place as yard work in the midst of suburban slaughter.

Yet focusing on the little pieces left by Hurricane Andrew is the only way to begin to understand. And, to begin to rebuild.

•

These Dade County cities, these homes, these belongings — these fragments that add up to nothing — lay scattered like the leaves of some hideous tree.

When Andrew crumpled the lives of his victims, he peeled away their grip on things, replacing it with his own fingerprints.

The familiar is strange in Andrew's new order; the usual, unusual.

In Coral Gables, at the Biltmore Hotel, relief workers are housed under the crystal chandeliers of that good-life landmark. In Florida City, Ronald McDonald, that bright yellow and red burger mascot, is draped in fatigues and shares a parking lot with a military command post.

And in Homestead, a Howard Johnson's motel has been turned into a clinic. Hand-printed labels mark "triage" or "pharmacy" on rooms where Keys-bound tourists were guests before Andrew. On U.S. 1, a spray-painted piece of plywood calls this "Ho Jo Hospital."

Even the dead are affected. Bodies waiting to be buried when Andrew struck had to wait a few days longer.

Postponed funerals. Curfews. Checkpoints. Unasked questions:

Where do a man and woman make love when their bedroom has been blown away? Where does a child learn to climb when the trees have fallen down? Except for the sameness of destruction, nothing looks the same: Regal palms are slammed to the grounds of Miami estates they once framed; avocado groves pruned by Andrew twist above fields in rural Princeton, like the dark roots of hell.

Nothing sounds the same: The thup-thup-thup of helicopters pulsates above quiet, empty suburbs.

Nothing smells the same: At Cutler Ridge Mall, birds rot in the wet heat. In Homestead and Florida City, the smell of decaying frozen food is mistaken for the reek of bodies.

Not even our senses make sense. There are few homesteads left in Homestead. There is very little "city" in Florida City.

A war veteran assesses the disorder:

"If we conducted a full-scale war here, it would not be as bad as what we see," says Sgt. Maj. Frank Mantia, of the 82nd Airborne, who served in the Gulf War. "I don't think there's any-

STRANGE NEW WORLD
Below: In Coconut Grove, two women run past a boat tossed on shore by the storm surge.

SEAN DOUGHERTY

thing in our arsenal that could do this.''

Hear Andrew's impact in the words of a policewoman, one of 10 Florida City officers who lost their homes.

"You need to get to the church? Go west on Palm Drive two main intersections and take a left where the 3,000 trailers used to be,'' says Sgt. Gail Bowen. "There is nothing but pieces of trailer. That is Redland Road, but you won't know that because there's no street sign.''

Hear what that means to people whose lives depend on order.

"I was chasing two looters last night,'' says Metro-Dade Police Officer Alex Ramirez, ''and I had no idea where I was. Normally, in a situation like that, you'd call for backup and give a landmark.

"But you can't give anybody a landmark, 'cause everything is stripped.''

When you do get directions, it might be an arrow painted on an ironing board or a message scribbled on a storefront.

People look for directions — and for answers.

Herman Wessel asks this as he stands in his broken home in Kendall: "What the hell can you do? You work all your life and then this. I mean you risk your life, and for what?''

DAWN OF A DARK MONDAY
On Fort Lauderdale Beach, a man leans into the wind and a police cruiser is stuck in a foot of sand washed ashore by Andrew.

LOU TOMAN

THE GROUND-ZERO EFFECT
Very little city remains of Florida City the day after the hurricane.

Everywhere, people ask: "Which way do we go?" Which way? When? Why?

•

A plus B equals C.

Usually, where there is a problem, there is a solution.

In the 20th century, knowledge and technology ensure our role as conquerers. No Ice Age wipes out generations. No plague kills entire populations.

Weather? Just a smiling paper sun or gray cloud on a TV forecast. At least in sunny South Florida.

Until Stormy Monday.

Aug. 24, 1992.

When Hurricane Andrew ravaged the southern tip of this state, it reminded us there are some things we cannot control, or quickly fix.

The most sophisticated weather-tracking equipment, hurricane experts and landfall odds-makers left South Florida with little more than 48 hours to prepare.

On Saturday, some residents scrambled to buy canned food, candles, plywood and jugs of water. Many even waited until the

following day to prepare or evacuate. Others did nothing at all.

"The storms usually peter out or go up the coast and hit North Carolina," says Helen Roth, of Deerfield Beach, on the Saturday before the storm. "If it hits, it hits. I guess I should go out and buy canned goods, but I haven't done anything."

This, as Andrew swirled 600 miles offshore, heading west for Miami.

A lot of us felt like Roth. Ten days before, after all, the storm was nothing but a West African puff. It nearly died 800 miles east of Florida. And it had been more than 50 years since the last Big Storm.

Even our preparations for Andrew seemed pathetic.

South Floridians criss-crossed windows with masking tape — as if Andrew's 140-plus mph winds could be stopped by sticky paper. Some seaside residents fled to friends' homes in western Dade — supposed havens that were among the hardest slammed by the storm.

Compared to the forces of nature, our knowledge meant

ROBERT DUYOS

A TEST OF FAITH
Daniel White, 9, sits in the wreckage of the Assembly of God church in Homestead. "I wanted the hurricane to come because I wanted to see how it would be," he said. "But now I don't have no home."

BY THE NUMBERS

- Damage in Florida: up to $20 billion.
- Homes destroyed in Florida, highest estimate: 63,000.
- Homes destroyed/damaged in Louisiana: 8,000.
- Damage per-capita for Floridians: $1,546.
- Insured losses: $7.3 billion.
- Expected insurance claims: 700,000.
- No power right after storm: 1.4 million homes.
- Left homeless: 250,000.
- Dead: 52.
Youngest: unborn male.
Oldest: 94.
Average age: 50.
Direct result of storm: 25; indirect: 27.
In Florida: 39.
Louisiana: 9.
Bahamas: 4.
How died:
Car crash, 2.
Crushed/trauma, 9.
Debris, 7.
Drowned, 7.
Electrocuted, 2.
Fall, 2.
Fire, 3.
Health-related, 12.
Plane crash, 2.
Tornado/lightning, 3.
Other, 3.
- Costliest storms:
1. Andrew, 1992, $20 billion.
2. Hugo, 1989, $7 billion.
3. Betsy, 1965, $6.3 billion.
4. Agnes, 1972, $6.3 billion.
5. Camille, 1969, $5.1 billion.
- Rank in deadliest U.S. storms: 23.

JACKIE BELL

SOUNDS OF WAR
The whirring of an Army helicopter above the ruins of Florida City adds to the sense of the surreal.

nothing. We knew, many of us, what a hurricane was. We knew about low atmospheric pressure and energy scooped from the warm ocean surface. We knew about counter-clockwise winds and the coding system used to gauge their strength.

We even named the monster, as we have for generations. It just seems more *controllable* if we give it a name.

Andrew. Sounds like a bratty child of Mother Nature.

Pick up your toys, Andrew.

"If he is going to take my place here, let him have it," says Charles Jones, a Florida City resident and father of five. "You don't have to tell me to get to no shelter no more."

"You will always ride through here and see the mark of Andrew," his neighbor, Leroy Byers, says. "It will be another 20 or 30 years before things get back to normal."

After Andrew threw a tantrum, and messed up his room — our room, our home — we felt helpless in our efforts to clean it up.

Sometimes modern technology — cellular phones and satellite dishes — is not as useful as a straw broom.

And even modern medicine wrestled to control the aftermath. With the contamination of water, and rotting piles of garbage, doctors faced the prospect of diseases found in the poorest countries: dysentery, diarrhea, cholera, typhoid.

Even a rusty nail could be deadly.

Medicine "is just something we took for granted. You could treat a nail puncture with one tetanus injection, one shot," said Emilio Menendez, a volunteer and nurse from Jackson Memorial Hospital, who ran out of shots. "But in this situation it is a serious problem."

•

Andrew created many serious problems.

When the winds came: Save your landscaping. When they increased: Save your home. When they gusted to 169 mph: Save your lives.

Like millions on the morning of

Aug. 24, Joe McCarthy tried to shut Andrew behind the doors of his home.

From room, to room, to room — through five bedrooms and nearly two hours of terror — Andrew chased Joe and his mother and sister through the Kendall home where Joe grew up.

"The storm would come into another room and we would get that door closed, and then we'd hear windows breaking," says McCarthy, 29. "It was sort of like somebody banging on the walls trying to get in.

"It was a personal kind of thing. Like, 'That storm is not going to come in and damage this place.' But now you realize there's nothing you can do anyway."

Robert Ramos tried to run.

LESSONS FROM OUR LOSSES
His cat, Dragon, was all Steve Saal had left, but Andrew threatened even that — officials would not let him take Dragon into a shelter for evacuees.

ROBERT DUYOS

Andrew beat the 40-year-old to death with flying debris.

Naomi Browning tried to hide. Andrew killed the 12-year-old with a beam in her bedroom.

Gladys Porter just wanted to be left alone. Andrew crushed the 91-year-old to death in the mobile home she refused to leave.

Ten days into the aftermath: Fifty-two dead. As many as 63,000 homes destroyed and 250,000 homeless.

Consider that last number.

> **'What the hell can you do? You work all your life and then this.'**
>
> HERMAN WESSEL
> of Kendall

More than the population of St. Petersburg, Fla.; approximately the size of Las Vegas, Nev., where odds-makers could have told you on Aug. 23 that Miami had a 23-to-1 chance of getting hit by Andrew.

Joe McCarthy is right. In Andrew's path, there was nothing you could do. But for thousands in his trail, survival is just beginning.

You can tack a shower curtain onto a torn roof. You can scavenge strips of somebody else's house from a lawn full of rubble and crudely patch your own. You can drag soaked belongings onto nail-littered lawns and pray for sunshine.

You can pick up a handful of leaves.

And you can reduce your feelings to large print and put them on the plywood that has replaced windowpanes and onto sides of homes where paint jobs no longer matter.

These are the spray-painted emotions from Hurricane Andrew:

"Let's work together. Andrew sucks the big 1."

"Looters! Loose stray dogs with AIDS inside. Will not bite State Farm adjuster."

"Coral Woods. An urban pioneer community by Arvida."

"Please help us Pres. Bush."

"Thank you Lord! This house may be down, but we're still around."

"Please send ice cream."

•

Hurricane Andrew showed us we could be jesters. We could be kind. We could be wicked.

Andrew showed us who we are.

Metro-Dade Detective Allen Davis knows. It's Wednesday, and Davis and his fellow officers are chasing looters from gutted stores along U.S. 1 in Cutler Ridge. His face is covered with razor stubble, his nerves exposed.

Davis' family lost five homes to the hurricane. Three of the four officers in his squad lost houses, too.

The officers' wives are home, with neighbors, picking scraps of pink insulation off family photos.

"I'm on the edge. I don't know whether to cry or go nuts half the time," Davis says, as he arrests two men stealing batteries and motor oil. "All of us have no houses. But we can't do anything.

"I have the patience of a match," he says.

Davis doesn't ignite. He does his job, one of hundreds of rescue workers, and storm victims, who helped others even when their own suffering made no sense.

Many helped.

Coconut Grove firefighters pooled $400 to buy chain saws to cut trees Andrew tossed onto streets.

Plantation cheerleaders raised $127 in a car wash, and got a

bank to match their donation.

A two-hour TV telethon raised more than $2.2 million.

Yet when Andrew exposed the guts of our houses, he also revealed our darkest corners.

A woman was arrested for cutting into a Miami ice line 5,000 people long.

A robber stole a family's $2,000 in insurance money after they lost their home to Andrew.

A Miami police officer trying to enforce curfew was shot in the head.

And, in the face of despair, some people were even petty.

A Lauderhill condominium board refused a resident's

JIM VIRGA

WHICH WAY DO WE GO?
**Three generations of one family
lost their mobile homes in Kendall.
Tamra Giffen comforts daughter
Catlin, 3, while grandmother
Dorothy Giffen rests on what was
left of a neighbor's home. Neither
family was insured.**

request to give haven to storm refugees unless he paid a $500 security deposit. The Cascades Condominium board wanted to make sure it covered possible damage to the lawns.

But, as officer Davis tells us, the worst of us are the thieves.

Disaster opportunists, some clustered along devastated roads, charged $3 for a loaf of bread; $1,300 for a generator that regularly cost $500; $5 for a pair of jeans, free at relief centers a few blocks away.

Some people simply take what they can. In disaster terms: Thieves become Looters.

In the war zone of U.S. 1 in Cutler Ridge, men and women dart past rifle-toting members of the National Guard, ducking into destroyed structures to loot stores where they once shopped.

"Your whole life is destroyed. And instead of helping, they are taking advantage of the situation," says Cindy Weeks, whose family owns a furniture store.

To stop thieves, Weeks negotiates with a vigilante in a white Camaro with an arsenal in his back seat.

Yet finding is not stealing, looters say. It is survival.

Bobby Borek sends his wife to cut into the front of food lines all over Cutler Ridge and Richmond Heights. He has a trunkful of food, and says he will keep going back.

"Those fools are wasting their time at the back of the line," says Borek, 34. "There won't be nothing left."

Nothing. Not even pride has a place in the world Andrew re-created.

Private homes become museums of devastation.

ANDREW'S TANTRUM
The storm surge and hurricane winds lifted the 210-ton freighter The Seward Explorer from
Biscayne Bay to Old Cutler Road, a distance of about 500 feet.

CARL SEIBERT

JOE RAEDLE

HELPING HANDS
In Homestead, paramedics rescue Tita Raime. She was stricken by heat exhaustion in her home, where there was no power and no air conditioning to fight off Florida's stifling summer.

See the family portraits. See the children's toys. See the name tags on work uniforms and know that Robert was a mechanic and that Betty did hospital volunteer work.

Walk into a Princeton neighborhood and stand over a pile of trophies. You've never met Bill O'Harris, but because of Andrew you know that in 1977 Bill's sports team voted him "the best coach."

Because of Andrew, we know the names of neighbors' insurance agents and their policy numbers, painted in foot-high letters over doorways.

Records, canceled checks, underwear. Intimate littered details are an unauthorized biography of families exposed by Andrew.

Andrew chased his humbled victims into food lines, where they bump together like cattle at the trough of a benevolent rancher.

"The only way to control the crowd," says National Guardsman Tim Cooke, on Day Two after Andrew, "is to tell them we're going to stop giving out food. That's the only way to get them to do what we say."

•

As big as Andrew was, when we saw the dawn of his devastation, we looked for something bigger. He took us on a journey of faith. God.

Andrew took Thelma Backert to church. It is the Sunday after the storm. She doesn't remember going to services in 71 years — since she was given a child's Bible at the age of 6.

"I never knew what this church was all about," says Backert, sitting in a pew at the First Baptist Church in Florida City. "I got a lot of feeling spilled out right now."

Family.

The storm brought James Mazyck home. He hadn't seen his mother in eight years.

"I was out on the streets

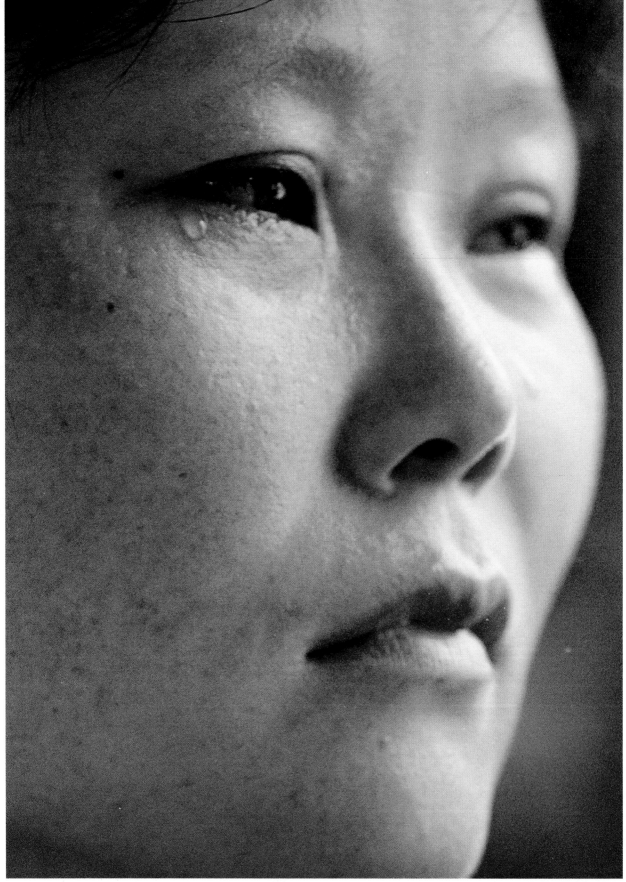

ELIOT J. SCHECHTER

A TEAR FOR GOD
Oki Raghunath weeps during a
Homestead church service six days
after the hurricane.

JOE RAEDLE

PRAYERS AMONG THE RUINS
St. Andrews Lutheran church in Homestead lost its roof, but not its faithful on the Sunday after Hurricane Andrew.

messin' with drugs and stuff," says Mazyck, as he patches Fannie Mae Mazyck's Florida City roof a week after Andrew. "The Lord touched me and told me to go home and be with my mama."

Society.

When Andrew destroyed order, he tested our faith in government. The one We The People created to insure domestic tranquility. To promote our general welfare. And secure those blessings of liberty.

Charles Jones, of Florida City, has only $50 left. Much of his roof is gone. His family is wet, hungry and afraid. He has no job, and no gasoline. Yet he hopes his government will provide.

"If the government could do what they did in Iran, or Iraq, there would be no problem," he says. "We'll survive if we can get some help."

Andrew even tested our faith in ourselves.

Maxine Parks does the best she can, fighting an angry food line in a grocery store parking lot. Her paralyzed son is at home, bed sores on his back, no water to wash him.

"That hurricane had a mind of its own. It was talking, talking," says Parks, of Cutler Ridge. "The way people live, it was letting them know we all have to work together. It is a message from Jesus."

Hurricane Andrew will be the turning point in many of our lives. For some of us, it will be the push down the stairs. The fall that ends up 10 years later in

ruined lives.

But others, like Pedro Vasquez and his fiancee, Julie Blair, believe it will be a new beginning.

Blair has a hard time getting child support from her ex-husband for her 3-year-old son. She and Vasquez lived together, with her family. They didn't like the Homestead trailer park. Too crowded. Too many fights and shootings.

Then came Andrew.

"We can clear everything out and start over," says Blair, 23. "It will get better."

When Andrew shook our world, he shifted our values.

Ask Al Harrison, who returned to his Kendall home to find his roof torn, but mostly intact. His house was flooded, but still there.

"A lot of small things simply won't seem that important," says Harrison, 66. "Being alive and

HANGING ON TO LIFE
The ballroom of the Biltmore Hotel in Coral Gables was transformed into a day care center for displaced city workers. Ashley Wiggins, 3, left, and Quanza Wiggins, 5, dance with city workers Mercy Ballina, left, and Michelle Basanez.

being able to help people rather than having things. Things can be swept away just like that.''

In our losses we found lessons. We learned the value of life, and of possessions. Ruined possessions — tinder for front-yard campfires, petri dishes for mildew — showed us Andrew's truth.

At the Coral Roc trailer park, John Hamley sees that truth in the waste left from decades of mobile-home life with his wife, Betty.

Betty collected ceramic figures, Haitian dolls. Each had a story. Now, sucked up and spit out by Andrew, the bits are simply part of the collective mess.

Betty says she won't start anoth-er collection. John says she will.

''She said, 'Oh my God, 44 years of possessions are gone. I thought, 'We started 44 years of marriage with nothing,'' John Hamley says. ''We can start all over again.'''

•

If Andrew taught us anything, it is this: Life is a series of challenges. And survival, simply hanging on.

A young woman wanders her ruined street. Looking down, she sees some small thing in the rubble. She bends down and picks up a little gray rabbit.

It is skinny and its teeth over-grown.

Maria Conde and a friend take the rabbit to a fast-food restaurant turned animal field hospital.

''We just feel bad for it,'' Maria says, laughing at herself. ''We're here worrying about a rabbit and we don't have a house.''

— *JOANNE CAVANAUGH AND JOHN HUGHES*

SHELTER FROM THE STORM
In Homestead, the Army set up tents for those whose homes were destroyed, but most stayed away to protect what was left of their property.

BY THE NUMBERS

- Category: 4.
- Eye size: 8-10 miles.
- Hours as a hurricane: 104.
- Rainfall, Miami International Airport, Sunday/Monday of storm: .33 inches. Next 10 days: 5.34 inches.
- Maximum gust: 169 mph, Key Biscayne.
- Maximum storm surge: 16.9 feet.
- Maximum sustained wind over water: 150 mph. Hitting land: 140 mph.
- Damage in Louisiana: $1 billion.
- Historically, drownings as percentage of all hurricane deaths: 90. Andrew: 13%.
- In South Florida shelters during storm: 84,000. Evacuated: 700,000. Refused to be evacuated: 300,000.
- New unemployment claims expected in Florida: 140,000.
- Free meals served within 10 days of storm: 1.7 million.
- Supplied by the military within a week:
  Helicopters: 98.
  Vehicles: 1,300.
  Meals ready to eat: 638,600.
  Portable radios: 15,500.
  Tents: 1,333 (enough to house 26,600 people).
  Portable kitchens: 30.
  Blankets: 100,000.
  Cots: 38,500.
- Traffic lights in Dade: 2,200. Still broken on Sept. 3: 1,258.
- Plywood sheets sold in one store two days before storm: 3,300. Promised for delivery next day: 7,500.
- Percent of 2,100 small businesses smashed in south Dade: 90.
- Red Cross expected to spend in Florida and Louisiana in 1992: $65 million.

A visual guide to Hurricane Andrew. Here are its path and how it compares to the four more-intense storms to hit Florida; the strength of its savage winds and the height of the "storm surge" wall of sea water; the path of its brutal center; and some of the places most affected by it or referred to in this book.

Most intense Florida hurricanes

Category 4 - 131-155 mph
Category 5 - over 155 mph

	Name	Year	Area	Category	Barometric pressure	U.S. deaths	Death toll rank (U.S. storms)
1	"Labor Day Hurricane"	1935	Keys	5	26.35	408	5th
2	Unnamed	1919	Keys	4	27.37	600-900	3rd
3	Unnamed	1928	Lake Okeechobee	4	27.43	1,836	2nd
4	Donna	1960	Entire state	4	27.46	50	21st
5	Andrew	1992	Dade County	4	27.52	48*	23rd

* not including 4 deaths in Bahamas

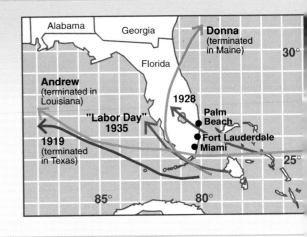

Wind and water

Top winds and "storm surge" – the wall of sea water created by Andrew – at various points.

Top wind gusts

1 Palm Beach International Airport
Top gust: 54 mph

2 Boca Raton Middle School
Top gust: 58 mph

3 Private home
Top gust: 90 mph

4 Goodyear blimp base
Top gust: 100 mph, then meter broke

5 Private home
Top gust: 105 mph; sustained winds 60-65 mph

6 Miami Beach
Sustained winds 85 mph

7 Miami International Airport
Top gust: 120 mph

8 National Hurricane Center
Top gust: 164 mph

9 Key Biscayne
Top gust: 169 mph

Water heights

A West side of Key Biscayne
Water height 4 feet

B Burger King Headquarters
Water height 16.9 feet

C Deering Estate
Water height 16.6 feet

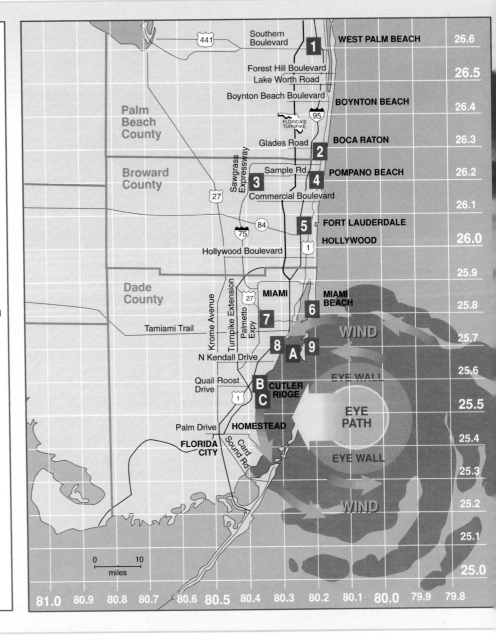

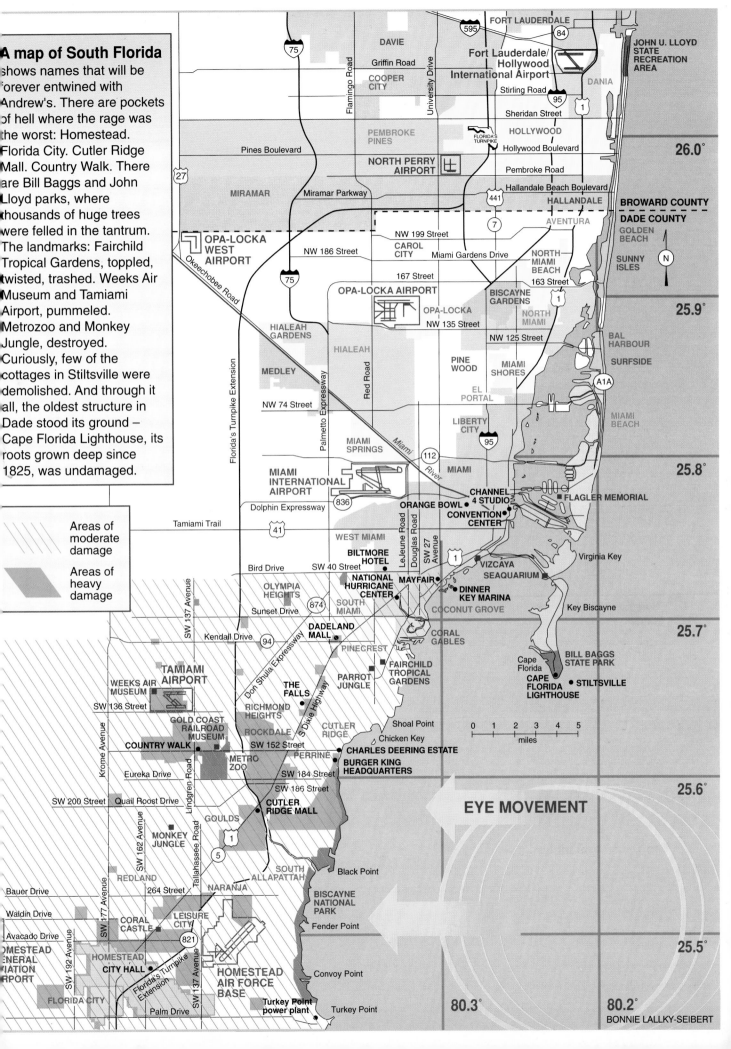

A map of South Florida shows names that will be forever entwined with Andrew's. There are pockets of hell where the rage was the worst: Homestead. Florida City. Cutler Ridge Mall. Country Walk. There are Bill Baggs and John Lloyd parks, where thousands of huge trees were felled in the tantrum. The landmarks: Fairchild Tropical Gardens, toppled, twisted, trashed. Weeks Air Museum and Tamiami Airport, pummeled. Metrozoo and Monkey Jungle, destroyed. Curiously, few of the cottages in Stiltsville were demolished. And through it all, the oldest structure in Dade stood its ground – Cape Florida Lighthouse, its roots grown deep since 1825, was undamaged.

Areas of moderate damage

Areas of heavy damage

FORT LAUDERDALE
DAVIE
Griffin Road
COOPER CITY
University Drive
Flamingo Road
Fort Lauderdale/Hollywood International Airport
DANIA
JOHN U. LLOYD STATE RECREATION AREA
Stirling Road
Sheridan Street
PEMBROKE PINES
FLORIDA'S TURNPIKE
HOLLYWOOD
Hollywood Boulevard
Pines Boulevard
NORTH PERRY AIRPORT
Pembroke Road
26.0°
MIRAMAR
Miramar Parkway
Hallandale Beach Boulevard
HALLANDALE
BROWARD COUNTY
DADE COUNTY
AVENTURA
GOLDEN BEACH
OPA-LOCKA WEST AIRPORT
NW 199 Street
CAROL CITY
Miami Gardens Drive
NORTH MIAMI BEACH
SUNNY ISLES
N
NW 186 Street
167 Street
163 Street
Okeechobee Road
OPA-LOCKA AIRPORT
OPA-LOCKA
BISCAYNE GARDENS
NORTH MIAMI
25.9°
HIALEAH GARDENS
NW 135 Street
NW 125 Street
BAL HARBOUR
SURFSIDE
HIALEAH
PINE WOOD
MIAMI SHORES
MEDLEY
Red Road
EL PORTAL
Palmetto Expressway
NW 74 Street
MIAMI BEACH
LIBERTY CITY
MIAMI SPRINGS
95
25.8°
MIAMI RIVER
112
MIAMI
MIAMI INTERNATIONAL AIRPORT
CHANNEL 4 STUDIO
FLAGLER MEMORIAL
Dolphin Expressway
ORANGE BOWL
CONVENTION CENTER
Tamiami Trail
836
WEST MIAMI
41
BILTMORE HOTEL
Bird Drive
SW 40 Street
LeJeune Road
Douglas Road
SW 27 Avenue
MAYFAIR
Virginia Key
VIZCAYA
SEAQUARIUM
OLYMPIA HEIGHTS
NATIONAL HURRICANE CENTER
DINNER KEY MARINA
Sunset Drive
874
SOUTH MIAMI
COCONUT GROVE
Key Biscayne
SW 137 Avenue
Kendall Drive
94
DADELAND MALL
PINECREST
CORAL GABLES
25.7°
Cape Florida
BILL BAGGS STATE PARK
Don Shula Expressway
FAIRCHILD TROPICAL GARDENS
CAPE FLORIDA LIGHTHOUSE
STILTSVILLE
TAMIAMI AIRPORT
WEEKS AIR MUSEUM
THE FALLS
PARROT JUNGLE
Shoal Point
SW 136 Street
RICHMOND HEIGHTS
S Dixie Highway
0 1 2 3 4 5 miles
GOLD COAST RAILROAD MUSEUM
ROCKDALE
Chicken Key
Krome Avenue
COUNTRY WALK
SW 152 Street
CUTLER RIDGE
CHARLES DEERING ESTATE
Eureka Drive
METRO ZOO
PERRINE
BURGER KING HEADQUARTERS
SW 184 Street
SW 186 Street
SW 200 Street
Quail Roost Drive
25.6°
CUTLER RIDGE MALL
EYE MOVEMENT
GOULDS
Lindgren Road
SW 162 Avenue
MONKEY JUNGLE
1
5
Tallahassee Road
SOUTH ALLAPATTAH
Black Point
Bauer Drive
REDLAND
SW 177 Avenue
264 Street
NARANJA
BISCAYNE NATIONAL PARK
Waldin Drive
Fender Point
Avacado Drive
CORAL CASTLE
LEISURE CITY
25.5°
HOMESTEAD GENERAL AVIATION AIRPORT
SW 192 Avenue
HOMESTEAD
821
Florida's Turnpike Extension
SW 137 Avenue
CITY HALL
HOMESTEAD AIR FORCE BASE
Convoy Point
FLORIDA CITY
Palm Drive
Turkey Point power plant
Turkey Point
80.3°
80.2°

BONNIE LALLKY-SEIBERT

ANATOMY OF A HURRICANE

PHIL SKINNER

A Spanish River Park ranger checks storm damage on the Boca Raton beach.

'A Mike Tyson Storm'

Andrew was conceived in a wind that swirled harmlessly thousands of feet above Dakar, Senegal. Then the swirls blew west, over the warm waters of the Atlantic Ocean near the Cape Verde Islands — the birthplace of killer hurricanes.

Tropical waves like this one come off the African coast once every three days or so. Why some survive and some don't is a mystery.

Andrew thrived. It fed on warm moist air that rose up its center, released heat and sucked up more humid air. A self-feeding process.

"It's a little bit of a cauldron that needs to remain intact," said Dean Churchill, a professor of meteorology for the University of Miami.

The cauldron kept on boiling. By Monday, Aug. 17, it had a name: Tropical Storm Andrew.

Gusts on Key Biscayne reached 169 mph and then broke the wind meter. At the hurricane center, top winds reached 164 mph and broke that gauge.

For the next few days, Andrew fought for its life against strong upper winds, which almost chopped the top off its center.

Andrew's cauldron nearly cooled and died.

The fight intensified on Wednesday — the day the Air Force Reserve sent its first plane to look for the center of the storm, but could barely find it. Meteorologists said if Andrew could last through Wednesday night, the upper winds would

leave and Andrew would live.

Andrew survived. By Thursday, the storm winds had died from 52 mph to 40 mph, but it was still a minimal tropical storm.

Andrew took nearly two days to recover from that fight. It was now Friday, Aug. 21. National Hurricane Center Director Bob Sheets that afternoon called local civil defense directors and said: Don't worry about the weekend. No hurricane warnings or watches will be needed until Sunday night at the earliest.

Sheets, a 55-year-old Midwesterner, was always the calm in any storm's eye. A dapper dresser with a TV smile, Sheets was not going to get wrinkled by a hurricane. He'd flown through too many, starting in 1965. Growing up in "tornado alley" in Indiana, Sheets became a hurricane expert working on his master's degree at the

HURRICANE ANDREW

AUGUST 24, 1992
0430 EDT

A satellite photograph from the National Oceanic and Atmospheric Administration shows the storm as it reaches land.

University of Oklahoma.

Sheets told civil defense officials: Don't worry quite yet. You've got time.

But time was not on the officials' side. Because of its compact size, Andrew sped up and intensified rapidly, surprising meteorologists. By Saturday morning, Andrew was a hurricane and getting more powerful by the minute.

Ever since it was born, Andrew had been heading in some kind of a westerly direction with a slight tilt north. But starting Saturday morning, Andrew headed only one direction: due west toward Dade County.

By 2 a.m. Sunday, Andrew was already a major hurricane with 120 mph winds. Nine hours later it packed winds of 150 mph, threatening to become the third most powerful hurricane to hit the United States.

"A Mike Tyson storm," said Gil Clark, a retired hurricane specialist who went back to work during Andrew. "It has a hard

blow, but it's not very big."

Sunday was a madhouse at the National Hurricane Center. TV crews spread out on the floor and Sheets, always calm, urged South Floridians to batten down and leave the coast.

And then the storm hit. Shortly after midnight the winds started. The hurricane center had shutters on all windows, but the wind whipped around the corner and sucked out one window despite the shutter. Floors and walls shook. The ceiling two stories above the hurricane center buckled. The building swayed.

Gusts on Key Biscayne reached 169 mph and then broke the wind meter. At the hurricane center, top winds reached 164 mph and broke that gauge.

All night, while Andrew smacked south Dade County, Lt. Col. Gale Carter, an Air Force meteorologist and veteran of 100 flights into hurricanes, was in the eye of the storm 10,000 feet above the ground. Fighting wind gusts of 255 mph, the plane lurched up and down hundreds of feet at a time. Lightning flashed and hail pounded the plane, peeling paint off its edges.

"We had severe turbulence," Carter said. "Severe means you have control of the airplane, but you can't read the instruments and have to be strapped in.

"One time during the breaks in the clouds, I looked out and I could see the street lights and I could see these blue flashes at random. They were power lines that were down and creating arcs. Just like flashbulbs going off at a concert. It was spectacular.

"That one mission was the roughest storm I've encountered," Carter said.

Unlike other hurricanes, Andrew did not slow down as it plowed over land. It was still able to feed on water in Florida Bay and the Everglades. It tore through Dade County, the Everglades and Marco Island.

By Tuesday morning, Sheets was on television warning Louisiana of the devastation to come. By this time, the always dapper Sheets had bags under his eyes. Two sets. The ever-present tie was gone. The shirt was wrinkled. He couldn't remember if he had slept since Saturday. His home was heavily damaged.

Andrew hit Louisiana with the same force it smacked into South Florida. Moving over the southeast United States during the next day, Andrew lost its status as a hurricane. But it remained a wet, violent storm. As a tropical depression, it still flooded areas, spawned tornadoes and toppled trees, killing a man in the Florida Panhandle.

Even after it was officially dead, Andrew was still a killer.

— *SETH BORENSTEIN*

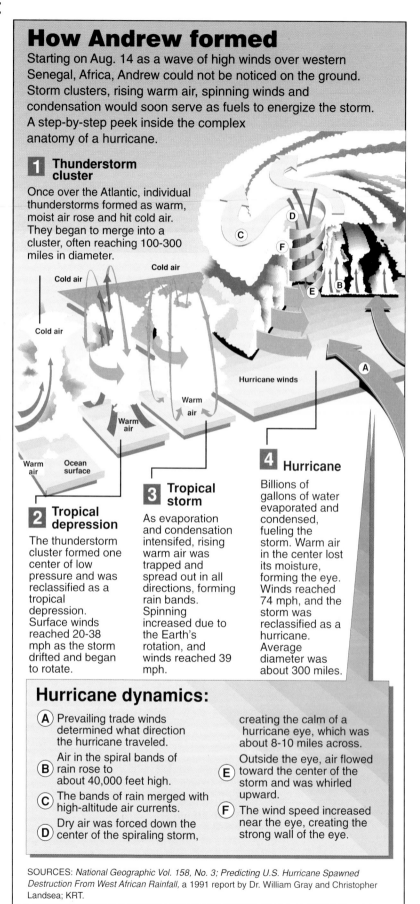

How Andrew formed

Starting on Aug. 14 as a wave of high winds over western Senegal, Africa, Andrew could not be noticed on the ground. Storm clusters, rising warm air, spinning winds and condensation would soon serve as fuels to energize the storm. A step-by-step peek inside the complex anatomy of a hurricane.

1 Thunderstorm cluster

Once over the Atlantic, individual thunderstorms formed as warm, moist air rose and hit cold air. They began to merge into a cluster, often reaching 100-300 miles in diameter.

Cold air
Cold air
Cold air
Warm air
Warm air
Warm air
Ocean surface
Hurricane winds

2 Tropical depression

The thunderstorm cluster formed one center of low pressure and was reclassified as a tropical depression. Surface winds reached 20-38 mph as the storm drifted and began to rotate.

3 Tropical storm

As evaporation and condensation intensifed, rising warm air was trapped and spread out in all directions, forming rain bands. Spinning increased due to the Earth's rotation, and winds reached 39 mph.

4 Hurricane

Billions of gallons of water evaporated and condensed, fueling the storm. Warm air in the center lost its moisture, forming the eye. Winds reached 74 mph, and the storm was reclassified as a hurricane. Average diameter was about 300 miles.

Hurricane dynamics:

(A) Prevailing trade winds determined what direction the hurricane traveled.

(B) Air in the spiral bands of rain rose to about 40,000 feet high.

(C) The bands of rain merged with high-altitude air currents.

(D) Dry air was forced down the center of the spiraling storm,

creating the calm of a hurricane eye, which was about 8-10 miles across.

(E) Outside the eye, air flowed toward the center of the storm and was whirled upward.

(F) The wind speed increased near the eye, creating the strong wall of the eye.

SOURCES: *National Geographic Vol. 158, No. 3; Predicting U.S. Hurricane Spawned Destruction From West African Rainfall*, a 1991 report by Dr. William Gray and Christopher Landsea; KRT.

ANDY DORSETT, LYNN OCCHIUZZO

The Music of Hell

Miami trembled.

Hurricane Andrew's early winds rattled the head of a street lamp near a downtown parking garage two blocks from Biscayne Bay.

It was a warning wrapped in a whisper.

In the next four hours, the whisper rose to a cry, the cry to a roar, and Miami became a city under siege.

At 2 a.m. Monday the rains began, gently at first.

Across from the garage, water dripped from the illuminated plastic Allright Parking lot sign and trickled off the glass roof of the Restaurante Brasileiro. The electric white lettering of the Miami Convention Center reflected on the damp street.

Waves of wind spit fiercer rains. Within an hour, three letters of the convention center's sign — C-O-N — began to flicker out like candles in a breeze.

By 3:24 a.m., no one who wanted to live ventured into the streets.

The storm hit Miami with a persistent fury. Downtown stoplights were knocked from their mountings, dangling by a single cord before crashing to the street. Metallic signs clanged and clattered, straining against their bolts. One broke loose and skated loudly over the pavement.

The sound of a hurricane is like the music of hell. Eerie, ghostly

URSULA E. SEEMANN

Reporter Bob Knotts chronicles the hurricane from a Miami parking garage.

whistles blended with a furious storm roar. The cracking of snapped metal pierced the hurricane's howl; unidentifiable objects popped and crunched in undetectable places. Somewhere, wood began breaking. The parking garage floor shook as though in an earthquake.

Ferocious winds bent and slashed trees, cracking off palm branches and skidding them into the blackness. A hotel awning tore into strips that flapped like shredded bedsheets.

At 5:21 a.m., Andrew pounded the city center. Years-old trees

broke in two and clogged the streets. Palm fronds curled into grotesque fingers that grabbed desperately at the wind.

Rain fell in a rage, a waterfall flipped on its side.

A metal grate bolted to the garage thrashed so frantically it bent a steel supporting bar. One of the grate's bolts popped off the concrete wall like a button from a shirt.

The Allright Parking sign was gone now, vaporized by the storm. So were dozens of glass roofing panels at Restaurante Brasileiro.

It was hard to understand how anything stood — why one stick of wood remained upright, why one post or pillar survived relentless Andrew.

When the wind died, the little things of everyday life — the newspaper rack, the stop sign, the tree on the corner — were still there. But the storm had tossed them in the air and dropped them in all the wrong places.

Yet the bricks and cement and steel that make up the city skyline stood as they did before the winds came.

Miami survived.

– BOB KNOTTS,
who, along with Senior
Photographer Ursula E.
Seemann, rode out Hurricane
Andrew in a Miami parking
garage near Biscayne Bay.

SEAN DOUGHERTY

Bryan Norcross, left, led anchors, including Tony Segreto, through the storm.

A Voice That Saved Lives

South Florida went to bed with the TV on. We wanted it on, just in case — advising us, calming us.

Perhaps that intimate knowledge of the storm that only TV had would reach us subconsciously while we dreamed.

The weatherman would reach out, rousting us with a tap on the foot. "Get up," he'd say. "Get out. Get in the car and drive away."

We had TV. We were safe.

All day Saturday we had been halfway listening to Channel 4. Every now and then, Bryan Norcross would pop up with an advisory, cutting into something like *NFL Milestone Men*. Soon

he was breaking in so often, the station gave him a permanent gig.

When, by 8:30 p.m., prime-time had vanished, we panicked.

We raided the cash machines. Gassed up cars. Called hotels.

There was something about the way Norcross was speaking that scared us. His tone. His messy hair.

Nothing about it seemed like regular TV. So there had to be something irregular en route.

By Sunday morning it was clear that some part of South Florida was going to be blown away. As we boarded up, we kept the weatherman on.

Should we flee west to the suburbs, or north past the county

line? How do we decide?

"If you're in an evacuation zone, please leave now," Norcross kept begging.

He was frightening. We hurried. It was almost 4 p.m.

We loaded cars with clothes, toys and enough food and water for two weeks, just like he said. Prepared to lose the house, we videotaped our big possessions, grabbed the house title, a wedding album and the baby books.

We were ready. But we didn't want to get in the car without that weatherman.

We finally found him on a radio simulcast. He said Interstate 95 was a mess. So we took another route. No traffic. We would make it.

Once again, we went to bed with the TV on.

We slept soundly at first.

Then a rock hit the window. Or something else.

But there was Norcross, still going at 5 a.m., hunkered down in what appeared to be a closet somewhere in the underbelly of his station. He was huddled with co-anchors Tony and Kelly, a bad light and (presumably) a camera operator. As always, he was dispensing advice. What to do. What not to do.

A panic-stricken woman from Kendall was on the phone. She said her roof was coming off. He told her to get away from all windows, crouch inside a bathtub and pull a mattress overhead.

He was saving lives.

We flipped the dial. Channel 7 was still there, its anchors also bravely tucked away in some

remote safe house, trying to look calm.

They didn't.

We wanted calm.

We searched for Ann Bishop. But she was gone. Replaced by a test pattern.

So we went back to Channel 4. We longed for daylight. We had to see what was out there. Soon there would be TV pictures.

They weren't too bad at first. A big tree on its side. A carport down. Then, as the news cars trickled down South Dixie Highway, the revelations began. A row of light poles, toppled in succession. Windows blown out. Walls missing. Then whole houses missing.

It took days to grasp the depth of Andrew's madness, during which TV assumed an unprecedented role in our lives.

The plastic hair and contrived jabbering had vanished. So had

almost all regular programming. Instead we saw reels and reels of sickening ruination. And heard hours and hours of endless conversation about it.

They taught us survival basics. How to safely handle a chain saw. How to purify water. How to deal with insurance people, banks and employers.

How to get a doctor, get a hot meal. How to volunteer, thwart looters, halt price-gougers.

How to live.

And in the absence of almost anything familiar outside our own front doors, we had Ann and Dwight and Bryan and Tony and so many others who became close friends. Just like the giddy station promos had promised for all those years.

TV won't look the same ever again. Nor will much of anything else.

— *DEBORAH WILKER*

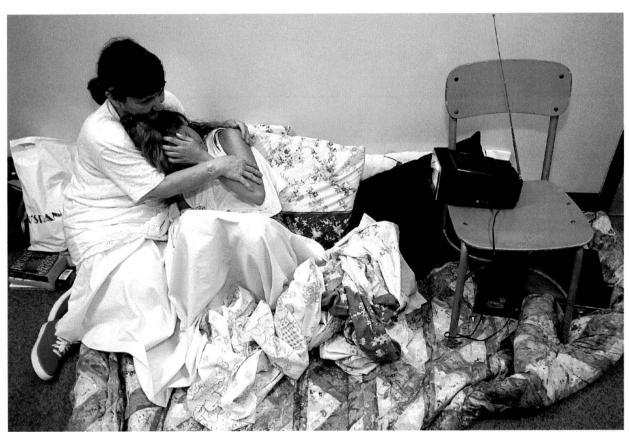

JACKIE BELL

Solange Orozco comforts her daughter Jessica, 14, at a shelter at Hallandale High School.

SEAN DOUGHERTY

People stand in line, some for hours, for a chance to buy ice from a semi-trailer parked near 184th Street and Florida's Turnpike.

The Second Disaster

It was two days since the nation's most destructive storm had laid waste to South Florida and as far as Mindy Gomez could tell, there was no one in charge.

A radio operator at Dade's Emergency Operations Center, Gomez found herself deluged with donated food and water — and with no way to get the desperately needed supplies to Andrew's victims.

The way Gomez saw it, Andrew had turned Dade's rescue center into a bureaucratic disaster area of exhaustion, frayed nerves, raging egos and meddling politicians.

Frantically searching for someone with enough muscle to get the stalled supplies moving, Gomez ran into U.S. Sen. Bob Graham en route to yet another news conference in which the public would be told help was on its way.

"They are on the verge of disaster in there," the Dade woman shouted at the startled senator, tears welling in her eyes.

"Don't they know people are dying out here? It takes forever for them to make a decision."

Bewildered, the senator scurried off to tell Andrew's victims to be patient.

•

Dade's disaster plan had worked well enough at the beginning.

As Andrew zeroed in on South Florida, some 100 emergency officials gathered inside a Civil Defense bunker built during the Cold War to withstand a nuclear attack, its 2-foot-thick walls massive enough to silence Andrew's fury as the storm pounded South Florida.

As Andrew drew closer, Metro-Dade emergency operations manager Kate Hale mused from deep inside her bunker, "It is

isolated in here.'"

Inside their bunker, Dade officials studied their hurricane plan.

It all seemed so simple:

The winds would subside.

Teams call in with damage reports.

Dade County Manager Joaquin Avino would make the key decisions, while Kate Hale would carry them out.

And if additional disaster aid was needed after the storm, Dade would have the final call on when, where and how to seek state and federal help.

The magnitude of Andrew's devastation began trickling into the bunker by radio and phone as the storm's winds receeded early Monday morning.

Yesterday's emergency paper drill had become a nightmare of devastation.

A city's worth of homes had been destroyed.

Residents of this Kendall home send out a desperate plea for aid.

Nearly all of Dade County had lost its electricity.

Communication by phone had become an impossibility.

The entire county's water supply had been contaminated.

Highways everywhere were blocked — a twisted tangle of trees, broken glass and dangerous power lines.

Armed looters plundered liquor, guns and appliances from ruined shopping centers.

Dazed and homeless storm victims stumbled about in search of food, water and shelter.

"We knew within hours that south Dade would literally have to be rebuilt from the ground up," Hale says, looking back. "It was just a staggering prospect.

"It is easy to go from A to Z in a book but when you're really doing it, things don't work out so easily."

The first problem, of course, was law and order.

The plan provided Dade County Police Director Fred Taylor with a response team of 1,500 officers. Roughly half the department. But hardly enough. Even with a backup of 2,000 National

JOHN CURRY

President Bush speaks to the media during his tour of Cutler Ridge on Aug. 24.

Next page: Cutler Ridge residents reach for food being given away by L&J Produce Co. of Miami.

SEAN DOUGHERTY

Guard troops.

"We're in a search and rescue mode," Taylor told the media. "We can't respond to anything else, except crimes actually in progress."

Thousands of Dade residents who dialed 911 after Andrew got a busy signal — or a frantic operator wanting to know how soon the party in trouble might die.

As the skies cleared, officials found it almost impossible to answer life-and-death calls, their fleet of emergency vehicles all but immobilized by traffic jams and deadly rubble. Even worse, the county's two rescue helicopters had been destroyed.

Andrew's tragic truth? In dealing with modern America's most destructive storm, Dade's emergency officials were like children battling a forest fire with squirt guns.

President Bush flew into South Florida to declare Broward, Dade and Monroe counties disaster areas within hours after the storm.

"Horrible," a stunned Bush mumbled as he toured the kindling and rubble.

"It looks like an atomic bomb went off," noted Florida Gov. Lawton Chiles.

Chiles and Bush promised immediate help for Dade's storm-crippled disaster team.

In the streets, chaos continued to reign.

"We are only responding to life-threatening emergencies ... and any crime in progress," Dade's desperate 911 supervisor said as Bush and Chiles toured ravaged south Dade.

"People ask us where they can buy gas, food and water," said Dade Fire Chief David Paulison. "The answer is, there's no place to do that."

Dade officials counted 50,000 homeless.

By Tuesday, the number of homeless had increased five times — with more than 250,000 storm victims lacking food, water and shelter.

By Wednesday, Dade's emergency boss Kate Hale was on the verge of enraged tears in her command bunker.

"Where the hell is the cavalry?" Hale snarled. "If we do not get more food into the south end [of Dade] in a very short time, we are going to have more casualties!"

President Bush had told state and local officials that help was on the way.

But as Federal Emergency Management Agency Director Wallace Stickney would later explain it:

"In any emergency, state and local agencies are on their own for a while. The federal government just can't be everywhere at the same time."

But Kate Hale and Andrew's 250,000 homeless victims were hardly on their own.

Thousands of Floridians had formed a massive army of guerrilla relief — starting convoys laden with tons of donated food, water and other emergency supplies.

Trouble was, the guerrilla relief convoys were blocked by massive traffic jams at turnpike and expressway exits leading into south Dade.

A few heart-breaking miles from the stalled relief convoys, storm victims fought over water and food.

"We need some type of coordination," said a Salvation Army captain in charge of mobile canteens.

Joe Greer, medical director of the Camillus Health Concern,

Christopher Castillo, 20, pleads with National Guardsman Russ Kaupp to let him get some food from a destroyed convenience store. Ray Luna, 22, needed the food for his baby, but Kaupp said he couldn't allow it.

JOE RAEDLE

Left: Kate Hale, head of Dade's Emergency Operations Center.

JACKIE BELL

Far left: Florida Gov. Lawton Chiles speaks to the congregation at Christ the King Church in Perrine.

SEAN DOUGHERTY

kept calling the state Department of Health and Rehabilitative Services.

"I had doctors, nurses, medications, medical equipment, everything, and nobody was interested," Greer says. "Nobody called me back. They were always having a meeting."

Meanwhile, back at Dade's emergency command post:

A representative of the Red Cross stormed back and forth, screaming that his agency was swamped with donations of food and that somebody had better rescue the Red Cross.

In another angry cluster, one Dade official engaged in finger-pointing with his bureaucratic counterpart from the Federal Emergency Management Agency.

And just down the hall, politicians took to the airwaves urging Andrew's victims to remain calm.

"Nobody is going to come to everybody with water and goods," explained Sen. Graham. "Initially, only the very severely in need are going to have people come to them."

In the end, it was Kate Hale's lonely task to try to explain the problem as she saw it three days after the storm:

"We have a catastrophic disaster," Hale said. "We are hours away from more casualties.

"We are essentially the walking wounded. We have appealed through the state to the federal government. We've had a lot of

people down here for press conferences. But [in the end] it is Dade County on its own.

"Dade County is being caught in the middle of something and we are being victimized," Hale cried. "Quit playing like a bunch of kids and get us aid. Sort out your political games afterwards."

The next day, President Bush dispatched 5,000 from the Army and 1,000 from the Marines — plus four giant field generators, 20 mobile kitchens, a half dozen field hospitals and a tent city for 20,000.

At the same time, state officials offered to share space with federal disaster officials at Miami International Airport to create a coordinated relief center.

U.S. Transporation Secretary Andrew Card flew into Miami to prod federal agencies into action.

Appearing before yet another swarm of cameras outside Card's government jet, a smiling Gov. Chiles told South Florida: "I think this might be the cavalry."

— *BUDDY NEVINS*

Gerry Trimble keeps watch over his property in Homestead. Many residents took up arms against looters.

SUSAN G. STOCKER

Metro-Dade sanitation workers haul away ruined clothing. Rainstorms in the days after the hurricane left many such donations mildewed and useless.

THE DEAD

TIM RIVERS

Funeral procession in North Lauderdale for John Michael Byers Jr., a firefighter/paramedic who was killed while working in Key Largo.

No One Was Safe

When daylight came that Monday morning, survivors began the cruel task of counting Andrew's dead.

It could have been worse. Evacuation saved many lives, as did the storm's southerly path, speed and minimal surge. The shelters helped, too, as did old-fashioned luck and the sheer fickleness of the wind. But lives were still lost, and Andrew was ruthless and indiscriminate in claiming its victims.

Ten days after Andrew, the death toll stood at 52 in Florida, Louisiana and the Bahamas.

No one had been safe. Andrew's victims ranged from an unborn child and a 12-year-old to three nursing home patients who died during evacuation to a logger struck by a tree in the Panhandle and a Palm Beach County teacher hit by lightning on a post-storm mission of mercy.

— *RAY LYNCH*

ANDREW'S DEATH TOLL

• In Broward: **John Stoian**, 41, and **Harold S. Kern**, 51, of Pembroke Pines, both in plane crash; **Richard C. Schaefer**, 57, chest trauma.

• In Dade: **Naomi Browning**, 12, hit by beam; **Vidal Perez**, 49, and **Francisco Sospedra**, 74, both thrown from a trailer; **Robert Moak**, 32, drowned; **Miguel Pulido**, 62, crushed; **Andrew Roberts**, 30, crushed; **Claude Owens**, 46, neck injury; **Robert Ramos**, 40, hit by debris; **Gladys Porter**, 91, crushed; **Mary Cowan**, 67, crushed; **Harry Boyer**, 67, crushed; **Jesse James**, 46, crushed; **Natividad Rohena**, 57, crushed; **Tommy Vann**, 36, drowned; **Edna Gerry**, 81, breathing problems; **Elaida Vargas**, 22, hemorrhage, and her unborn male child; **Jose Saravia**, 73, heart attack; **Dagoberto Troya**, 50, heart attack; **Alvia Cruz**, 80, died during evacuation; **Manuel Rodriguez**, 69, **Fannie Lytle**, 94, and **Anice Berett**, 81, died during evacuation; **Emma Grace Parker**, 74, fall; **Anthony Margiotta**, 79, fall; **Herman**

Lucerne, 78, heart attack; **Shabonnie McKenzie**, 9, and her cousin, **Dominique Seymour**, 6, both fire; **Anthony J. Pastor**, 40, electrocuted; **Kathleen Robinson**, 63, heart attack; **Richard Kuzina**, 66, heart attack; **Frederick Stone**, 40, heart attack; **Jacqueline Parker Koger**, 43, car accident; **Herbert Engleman**, 55, lightning.

• In Monroe County: **John Michael Byers Jr.**, 22, head injury.

• In North Florida: **Henry Waylon Bush**, 41, hit by debris.

• In Louisiana: **Carlos Cabrera**, 63, LaPlace, tornado; **Mervin L. Sevario**, 34, Denham Springs, electrocuted; **Jessica Tomlinson**, 2ü, LaPlace, head injuries; **Tuan Hoang Le**, 33, **Sau Van Duong**, 26, and two unidentified bodies found in Gulf of Mexico; **Vivian Decuir**, 50, Abbeville, car accident; **Allen Stewart**, 86, fire.

• In Eleuthera, the Bahamas: **Telford Neely**, 16, **Avaro Pedican**, no age given, **Beverly Moss**, no age given, all killed by flying debris; and **Yvonne Cash**, 37, drowned.

LOU TOMAN

T.J. Durand, 4, of Oakland Park drops off a bottle of water at a collection site.

Miracles From Disaster

We're from Haiti, Cuba, Peoria, the Bronx. Hurricane Andrew was the first thing in years to bring us together.

Nature turned on us.

Government failed us. But we didn't fail each other. Andrew tore up lives, but, damn those 160-plus mph gusts, we fought back with bootstrap heroism.

And, in Andrew's twisted legacy, we became a community at last.

We didn't wait for the president to send in troops. We couldn't. Death had brushed its fingers through our hair. That could have been me, we whispered.

Andrew carved a circle where there had been nearly impenetrable lines. The circle began small, in places where people stepped

from their homes at dawn and discovered ruin.

The circle grew when more than 2 million others awoke, thankful for their lives, then saw the sickening footage on TV. Streets of mangled wood and metal, the stuff of families' homes. Florida's green horizon, stripped. And the people: Could these be Americans? They looked like dazed refugees. The images broke hearts, then opened them wide.

And out of the rubble rose heroes big and small.

Who could forget John Stoian and Harold S. Kern, the two Broward County men who died after their twin-engine plane — packed with supplies for victims — crashed into a Miramar home?

"He just wanted to help," said

widow Lucy Stoian, fighting tears.

Then there was Herbert Engelman, who left his home in Lake Worth to set up an emergency radio center in the ruins of Homestead. Ignoring a storm rumbling overhead, the Palm Beach County teacher continued to work on his radio equipment until a bolt of lightning struck him dead.

"He was a doer," his brother-in-law said. "He just wouldn't stop."

Downwind from Andrew, it's hard to explain all the hurricane did. Sure, its evil is everywhere. But so is our basic human good.

County lines vanished as South Floridians launched a massive guerrilla relief effort. Hundreds, perhaps thousands, of people

NICHOLAS R. VON STADEN

drove toward the devastation with bottled water, canned food, diapers, plywood. They clogged every highway. A 10-mile drive took two hours, inch by excruciating inch. Nails punctured tires. They pressed on. When they reached south Dade, what they saw shook their souls.

"It becomes surrealistic after a while," said Cynthia Lowen, a Delray Beach volunteer, as she stood in a wreckage of mobile homes.

Said Lisa Parks, a spokeswoman for the United Way, "No one was prepared for a catastrophe of such major proportions, or for the size of the outpouring."

The outpouring, so vast it was impossible to measure, included much more than food and water. People trucked in portable toilets, restoring some dignity to homeless people in fields. Police in Coral Springs loaned cars to officers in Florida City and Homestead. Volunteers flooded in from Georgia, the Carolinas, Virginia, Canada.

As health officials warned of possible outbreaks of typhoid and cholera, troops of volunteer medical workers and teams of

psychology professors ventured to Andrew's victims. Their mission: to treat ailing bodies and grieving hearts.

"I'll be honest with you," said volunteer Dr. Pedro Jose Greer Jr. of Coral Gables. "I feel scared and a little overwhelmed."

Andrew scared us, overwhelmed us — and galvanized us. One man drove all the way to Georgia to pick up 43,200 pounds of ice. "I didn't know where I was going," he said. "I just knew people needed ice."

When emergency officials begged people to stop clogging Dade roads with convoys of good intentions, people unloaded supplies at their local malls, work places, fairgrounds and rail stations. "Call me your basic American who wants to volunteer," said Lake Worth resident John Hiley. "Somebody's got to do it. Forget the government."

What government couldn't do immediately, people did. Politicians were humbled. "God bless the volunteers," George Bush said outside Homestead's ruined city hall.

Andrew awakened in us an insatiable desire to give. And the less fortunate

JUDY SLOAN REICH

SUSAN G. STOCKER

CARL SEIBERT

SUSAN G. STOCKER

Above: Rick Barrett and John Burkhart load relief supplies onto a helicopter at Fort Lauderdale Executive Airport.

Above left: Kerri Kehril of Lauderhill sorts clothing at a Coral Square mall relief center.

Left: Judy Lyons of Davie rallies relief volunteers at the Broward Mall.

Far left: Jeff Pinder of Boca Raton helps build a temporary roof for a Homestead resident.

among us were thankful. "Thanks ain't enough," one of Andrew's victims told a TV reporter. "But it's all we've got."

When a group of TV stations held a telethon for hurricane victims, people called at a rate of 125,000 an hour. Not all got through, but the telethon netted $2.2 million in pledges.

High school cheerleaders from Plantation washed cars, earned $127 and learned that Barnett Bank would match their donation to the Red Cross. All over, banks, corporations, churches, social groups, military organizations and private institutions opened their own wallets to help. Winn-Dixie supermarkets trucked in nearly 250,000 gallons of water.

When it seemed that Andrew's victims had nothing left to give, they gave. George Diaz loaned his damaged house in Homestead to Hialeah's Palmetto General Hospital, which set up a field hospital. Where Diaz and his family once ate dinner, hospital workers opened a pharmacy.

Tessie Lopez invited 25 people to sleep on her living room floor. After all, she had the only roof in her neighborhood near Homestead. "I turned the floor into a motel," she said.

Near Perrine, people will remember Clint Smith for his meat — all $500 worth, thawing in his powerless freezer until he shared it. Hungry neighbors ate chicken, steak and ribs cooked on a barbecue.

"Nobody will go hungry with Clint around," one woman said.

So, in Andrew's wake, we feasted on human kindness. The circle was complete, a miracle from a disaster: South Florida had found a connection to itself.

— *MELINDA DONNELLY and*
JILL YOUNG MILLER

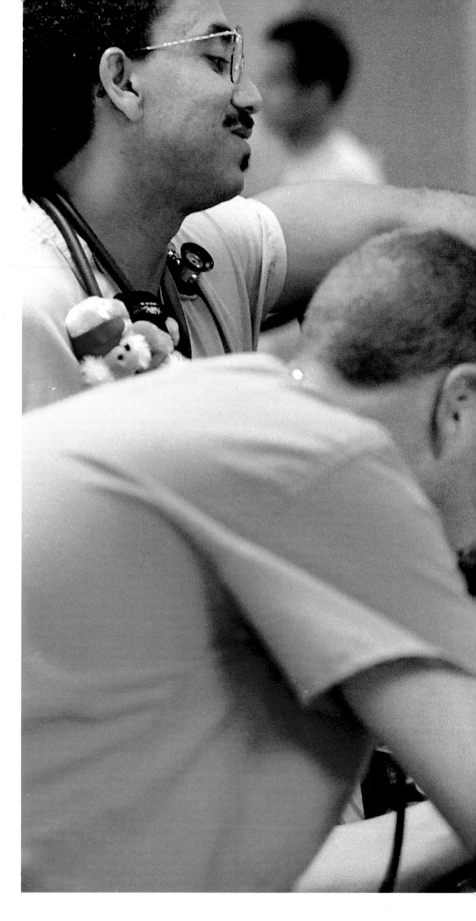

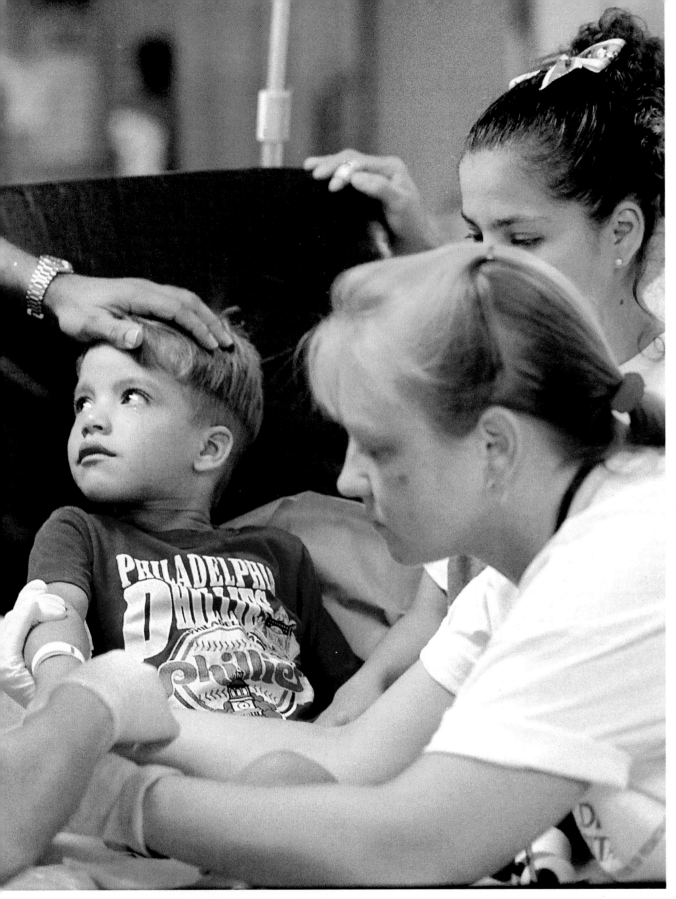

Raymond Cruz, 6, of Homestead receives a smile from Dr. Luis Bauzo as nurses Victor Ceilo, left, and Cindy Garlesky insert an IV. Mom Madeline Cruz looks on.

CARL SEIBERT

JOE RAEDLE

National Guard Sgt. Steven Malvita, right, makes an arrest with the help of a paramedic. The suspect was found taking merchandise from a Homestead store.

Looters and Hustlers

Hurricane Andrew brought out the best in most of us — and the very worst in a few.

Our dark side first showed itself as Andrew bore down and we ran to buy plywood, batteries and bottled water, often paying three times the price to hustlers eager to cash in on our fears.

Then came Andrew's devastation at daybreak — followed by roving bands of looters dashing into wrecked buildings for armloads of clothing, appliances and liquor.

In malls, record shops, liquor stores, groceries and electronics stores from Coral Gables to Florida City, it was like an insane party as laughing thieves helped themselves.

Police officers raced through littered streets and ruined homes to aid the injured, sick and elderly victims of the storm.

"Frankly, the priority is not property, but life," Pat Brickman, Metro-Dade police spokesman, said as looters pillaged south Dade's storm-ravaged shops. "We're handling life-threatening situations."

National Guard units joined police to battle the mini-army of looters.

"There were about 100 looters all over this mall when we got here," said Guardsman Pfc. Eric Henderson. "There were young people, old people, people with little kids. We caught them in the act and they took off running. We didn't try to detain them."

Looters swept through the wreckage in two waves.

First came society's renegades, needing little, or no excuse to break the law.

Next, homeless storm victims who stole food and water to ease their hunger and thirst.

One image after the storm: His name is Christopher Castillo, the young man says, and he hasn't seen a relief truck or had a hot meal for days. He's eating the only thing he could find to steal from a Homestead convenience store — Rolaids.

A National Guardsman catches Castillo pawing through the rubble, still chewing Rolaids.

"Please, please, you don't understand," Castillo tells Spec. Russ Kaupp. "I need food. I need milk for my cousin's baby. We

PRICE GOUGING

How prices in some cases changed after the storm:

Plywood
Before: Less than $10 for 4-by-8 sheet.
After: $20 to $40.

Tree trimmer estimates
Before: Free.
After: $25.

Chain saws,
16-inch.
Before: $139.
After: $250.

Generators,
4,000 watt.
Before: $488.
After: $2,000.

Bread
Before: $1.09.
After: $3.

Adult diapers
Before: About $40.
After: $100.

Ice
10 pounds.
Before: $1.39.
After: $10.

An ice company employee sells bags of ice out of the back of his truck to people in Kendall. He had just completed a scheduled delivery and was selling the leftovers.

ANDREW ITKOFF

Miami police arrest a woman at the Royal Palm Ice Co. Police said she cut into the line, which had about 5,000 people, and disobeyed police orders.

have nothing, man. You don't understand. What can I do?"

But Kaupp has a job to do.

"I'm in a bind. I can't let you do this. It's not right," the Guardsman tells Castillo.

In the end, Kaupp is moved to free Castillo. But it troubles him.

"Our hearts may be moved to the very depths," Kaupp says. "But without law and order, there is anarchy."

By Tuesday, National Guardsmen were posted at shopping malls, major department stores and around walled-in residential communities.

Business owners hired security guards and vigilantes armed with semi-automatic pistols and sub-machine guns.

In many neighborhoods still without troops or police, home-owners walked the streets with rifles, shotguns and pistols — having scrawled signs warning looters they would be shot, or bitten by AIDS-infected dogs.

"I had to get out my shotguns because people were coming up to my house," said Robert Olsen of South Miami Heights. "We already had to chase two people away."

"People are holding guns at their homes," said JaLynn Hollis as she stood in the ruins of her Homestead trailer. "We lost almost everything and people take what little else we do have."

Price gouging continued for several days after Andrew. Hustlers dealing from the backs of trucks and some greedy store owners took their pound of flesh from desperate storm victims.

It was four days before the first waves of regular Army and Marine units rolled in to bring basic law and order to the ruins.

Food looting halted as victims found hot meals and clean water at Army field kitchens.

Business owners began boarding up ruined shops, while armed troops guarded malls.

Price-gouging abated as Florida Attorney General Robert Butterworth sent in a team of investigators to issue subpoenas.

A week after Andrew, police had arrested 184 storm burglars and looters.

Dazed, many storm victims moved north to find temporary shelter in Broward and Palm Beach counties — only to encounter a new breed of thief.

Tommy Wagner sent his wife, Lisa, and two children to a Fort Lauderdale beach hotel while he stayed behind with a gun to guard the ruins of their Cutler Ridge home.

Lisa and her children had just checked into the hotel when a stranger with a gun forced his way into their room and stole their emergency insurance money.

"If I was there when that guy came in," said Tommy Wagner, "he would have been dead."

— *KEVIN DAVIS*

JOE RAEDL

Elsa Merino refuses to leave her store; she asked Homestead police for protection from looters but was turned down.

THE CHILDREN

SUSAN G. STOCKER

Steven Adams, 6, is cradled by his mother, Micha, camping out in Homestead.

'I Hate Andrew'

It's the world of a child's drawing:

Homes now empty boxes, with crooked walls and missing doors and roofs that aren't quite there.

Trees they used to climb now leafless, limbless stick figures against the sky.

It's a different kind of world, but one that's all too real for the thousands and thousands of children whose lives have been changed forever by something they call, simply, Andrew.

"I hate Andrew," Shaquanda Pate says in the angriest tone a 10-year-old can muster. "He left us nothing but junk."

Nothing but junk.

Just ask Curtis Walker, 10, standing outside what's left of his home in Goulds as he surveys his shattered neighborhood.

"It looks ugly," he whispers, disappointment in his voice and a blank, distant look in his brown eyes. "There's my roof over there by that tree."

Curtis remembers standing in a tiny room with nine family members. His mother went away for a while. He recalls thinking: "I hope my mommy's not dead." Then the roof blew away and he heard a painfully piercing sound, like "someone whistling really loud."

"I just wanted it to stop," Curtis says. "I wanted it to stop."

Each child has a story to tell about the storm and what they saw. But ask about the future — where they hope to go from here — and there is no answer.

Many speak of nightmares.

"The most important thing for all of them who have undergone the trauma is that they have an opportunity to express their feelings," says Dr. Helen Orvaschel, associate professor of psychology and director of the child and adolescent depression program at Nova University.

"They need a chance to repeat it," she says. "To go over it."

Eddie Fulton wants to talk. He'll tell you he was in a closet with his family. Praying. "Please, God, please let us live through this. This isn't happening. This isn't really happening."

"I thought this kind of thing only happened on TV," the 14-year-old from Naranja says.

Marlow and Merrie Christi Boylan had their own rooms in a middle-class neighborhood in Homestead. Though their house still stands, their rooms are gone.

"We were lucky, though," Marlow, 15, says of himself and

Latasha Walker, 8, in the church next door to her home in Goulds.

JACKIE BELL

Jose Delion, 12, from the migrant camp in Florida City, picks up food and water for his family.

his 16-year-old sister. "My friend Eric, he watched his roof float away."

"My next-door neighbors, they don't have no family around," says Diana Mejia, 9, from Cutler Ridge. "At least we got relatives."

Latasha Walker, Curtis' sister, worries about her grandmother and all the things that used to be so pretty in her grandma's house.

"I felt real sorry when I went to her house and saw how Andrew messed everything up," the 8-year-old says breathlessly. "I gave my grandma a little glass heart with flowers on it for her jewelry. It cost 7 dollars and 15 cents."

The child searched the ruins of her grandmother's home for the gift she'd given the older woman.

"I found it," the child says. "It had just some scratches, but it wasn't broken. It made me smile."
— *BERTA DELGADO*

Left to right: Patricia, 3, Mindi, 7, and Jennifer Trimble, 8, with Steven Adams, 6, play on an uprooted palm tree in Old Hartford Square, Homestead.

We Will Survive

Andrew had passed and we emerged from our hiding place, shaking with fright.

Our roof was gone. Almost everything we owned was drenched and dirty.

We laughed.

My husband, Michel, and I put our heads back and laughed — not bitter chuckles, but true guffaws of joy.

We had survived.

We live in the Pinecrest neighborhood in Dade County, the northern fringe of the area hardest hit by Hurricane Andrew.

Andrew had burst through our French doors and peeled away our roof. Wind roared through our house, threatening to explode all our windows.

We grabbed our children — Benjamin, 5, and Ayla, 1 — and took refuge in a bathroom. We crouched on the floor, holding the door closed against the wind. Benjamin was so overwhelmed that putting his head under a pillow with his hands on his ears was not enough; I had to put my hands over his or he would panic and scream.

Five days after the hurricane, we returned to what was left of our house.

The joy of surviving had worn off. Now we were faced with impossible tasks. Where should we start the cleanup? Where will we live?

We shouted at each other, at

KiKi, Michel and son Benjamin with dog at their Dade County home.

the children. Ayla whined endlessly; Benjamin cried at the drop of a hat. He punched me more than once.

For days, Benjamin refused to return to our house. He insisted on being left behind at Grandma's.

On this day, however, he decided it was more important to be with us. He was in his bedroom, sorting his toys, when all of a sudden he came flying out. He was crying hysterically.

Through the window, he had seen lightning from a far-away rainstorm. He thought another hurricane was coming.

By the time we began searching for a new place to live, there was little left. I called friends, real estate agencies and every ad in the paper, getting more and more desperate.

"I have two kids," I would say, hoping to gain sympathy. But the few houses that were available were being rented over the phone, sight unseen.

Then I found a three-bedroom home not too far away. There were four people ahead of me on the waiting list. I knew it would be gone after the first person saw it. So I did something I will forever be ashamed of. I bribed the owner $200 a month to let me see it first. I told him — and myself — that I had to do whatever it took to help my family.

I even apologized to him for making the offer.

He apologized for accepting it.

The house was just right for us. As Michel and I huddled in a bedroom trying to figure out how to come up with $18,000 for the six-month advance rent, the family that was supposed to be first on the list drove up.

The husband jumped out of his pickup truck. The wife followed, clutching the newspaper. They looked as desperate as we felt.

We walked away from the house.

Someday all this will be over. On that day, I want to be able to celebrate how we got through the crisis with strength and dignity.

I can find another house. It is more important that I be able to live with myself.

– KIKI BOCHI,
a former writer and editor
for the Sun-Sentinel.

MIGRANT WORKERS

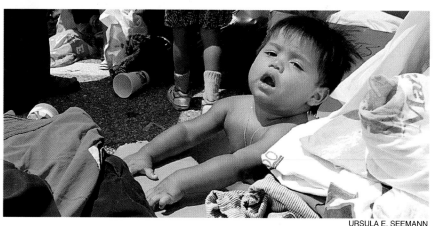

URSULA E. SEEMANN

Felipe Duenes, 1, sits in a cardboard box while his mother looks for clothing at the migrant camp in Florida City.

Harvest of Sadness

Long before Andrew's devastation, migrant life in rural south Dade County was a far cry from the American Dream.

A typical migrant family of four earns about $8,000 a year picking winter vegetables and fruit, or toiling in the region's nurseries.

Rent is $52 a week for a battered trailer or ramshackle home.

While feeding America, migrants buy their groceries with food stamps.

Families are forced to move every few months to follow the harvest season.

Florida's planting season had just begun when Andrew tore across the rich farmland, leveling three migrant camps in south Dade and leaving some 1,000 farmworker families homeless.

Losing their homes proved a tragic prelude to a season of grief for the farmworkers.

Andrew's cyclonic winds and salt-laden rain destroyed a sea-

son's worth of crops.

"I don't think there's going to be any work for them for a long time," says Susan Reyna, deputy director at the Centro Campesino farmworker center.

"Los rancheros [the farmers] say there will be no work for us this year," says Jesus Munoz, 28, who has been picking vegetables since he was 7.

Andrew turned his trailer to kindling and left his family of five homeless.

"Se acabo el mundo [It is the end of the world]," Munoz says.

Struggling to survive in a world of contaminated water, poor sanitation, heaps of rotting garbage and half-inch-long mosquitoes, the rural poor are potential victims of Third World diseases.

"I know the water was bad," Munoz says. "My daughter had diarrhea from it."

Doctors are treating victims like Munoz's daughter for everything from diarrhea to rashes — as

public health officials braced for cases of typhoid or cholera.

Most of the farmworkers are reluctant to leave the land they have worked for so many years.

Reyna and other farmworker officials hope the camps will be rebuilt; the fields are there and next year will bring a new crop.

"The people need financial resources to determine what they're going to do," she said. "There are so many who are homeless."

In the days following Andrew, relief trickled into the ravaged rural fields.

Pam Benson and her husband saw the devastation on television in Tampa.

They loaded $500 in groceries into their 1981 Lincoln and set off for south Dade.

"These are America's forgotten people," said Pam Benson. "They put food on our tables, but nobody ever thinks of them."

— *KATHLEEN KERNICKY*

Patricia Kale and Deon Smith, 12, cool off at a fire hydrant in the Sunny Gardens area of Perrine.

JOHN CURRY

Joan Poirier, Gregg Petronela and Suzanne Bedard huddle around a hurricane lamp in Poirier's Fort Lauderdale home the day after the hurricane knocked out the electricity.

Danger in the Dark

When the sun sets on Gerry Trimble's stricken neighborhood, the darkness becomes a new enemy to conquer.

Trimble, his wife, two dogs, three kids and assorted neighbors turn his front yard into a community campground. No one wants to risk sleeping in the caved-in remains of their homes. Besides, it feels safer in numbers.

In the dark, the fallen trees and roofless, shattered homes take on a sinister appearance. Anyone approaching Trimble's home had better say who they are or they risk being shot with his Winchester rifle.

An ancient gas lantern that gathered dust in Trimble's garage is brought out on the third night after the storm. He's tired of spending the nights camped out in his front yard with the stars as his only light.

Chung, Trimble's wife, warms up packets of ramen noodles one at a time on a Korean camp stove. This is how every meal since the storm has been served.

In the distance, the hum of gasoline-powered generators and neighbors talking and laughing wafts through the night air.

The people of south Dade — particularly Homestead and Florida City — face being without power for months and maybe years. The delicate framework that acts as a conduit for electricity was smashed in the storm.

Restoration of power has been a gradual process for the 2,900 Florida Power & Light Co. workers stationed in Broward and Dade counties. Even though several hundred FPL workers lost their homes, the employees labor around-the-clock.

To help their fellow electrical workers, crews from North Carolina and Mississippi have pitched in — many from the same crews that restored power to storm-ravaged Charleston after Hugo three years ago.

But danger is everywhere in the dark.

During the first week of work, three FPL workers are burned by electricity fed from a portable generator into a downed power line.

Six days after the storm, Juanita Seymour still lacks power in her north-central Dade home. She leaves a candle burning for a family member coming home late at night.

The candle sets the house afire, killing two children, 9-year-old Shabonnie McKenzie and 6-year-old Dominique Seymour. Juanita Seymour is seriously injured.

— DONNA PAZDERA

SUSAN G. STOCKER

Hyon Mealy falls asleep by candlelight in front of neighbor Gerry Trimble's house in Homestead on Aug. 27.

JOE RAEDLE

Storm-torn power lines are worked on in Homestead.

HOW POWER WAS RESTORED

Here is a chronology of how power was restored to Dade, Broward and Palm Beach counties:

Monday — 1.4 million homes without power on Florida's east and west coasts.

Tuesday — 773,500 without power, including 640,000 in Dade County, 132,000 in Broward County and 1,500 in Palm Beach County.

Wednesday — 585,000 without power, including 506,000 in Dade and 79,000 in Broward.

Thursday — 389,000 without power, including 334,500 in Dade and 55,000 in Broward.

Friday — 367,000 without power, including 330,000 in Dade and 37,000 in Broward.

Saturday — 325,000 without power, including 300,000 in Dade and 25,000 in Broward.

Sunday — 287,000 without power, including 275,000 in Dade and 12,000 in Broward.

JOHN CURRY

Troops march out of a C5A Galaxy at Homestead Air Force Base.

To the Rescue

When Hurricane Andrew marched ashore it was no sneak attack. We watched its formation for days. We sent spy planes behind enemy lines to measure its size and strength. We monitored its advance by longitudinal degree.

We knew that unlike other hostiles, there was no way to battle him, save hunkering down and preparing for the worst. We figured the enemy would come and go and we'd be done with him.

South Florida's National Guard, our first line of defense, was activated early to thwart looters and help direct traffic. They were 1,000 strong.

But when dawn broke on Monday and the first hand-to-hand combat began, arresting a few looters would end up being a minor diversion.

The militia was fighting an enemy that no one was trained to battle: the hunger, thirst and collective pain of a quarter-million people.

The Guard was quickly overrun. A call went out for more National Guard units. Their number would grow to 6,000.

For the next few days the battle revealed an enemy both pervasive and wicked. Andrew had put up roadblocks — trees and parts of shattered buildings in the streets. It had strung electric wire — downed power lines draped across neighborhoods. It left behind booby traps — partially destroyed roofs and teetering poles threatening all relief efforts. Reinforcements were badly needed.

Who asked for what and when they asked for it will long be debated. But the sound of the cavalry was heard at daybreak on Friday, five excruciating days after the storm.

At 8:05 a.m., the first federal troops from Fort Bragg, N.C., rolled onto a Homestead Air Force Base tarmac that hours before was strewn with the remains of an obliterated military installation.

The new troops joined the ranks of the stunned.

"This is worse than anything we saw in Saudi," said Master Sgt. Lester Richardson, who had spent six months in the Middle East during Operation Desert Storm. "These people need a miracle."

They could not produce a mira-

Left: National Guardsmen keep people in line as they wait to buy ice from a semi-trailer parked near 184th Street and Florida's Turnpike.

SEAN DOUGHERTY

Below: A National Guardsman points the way to an exit from a Publix food giveaway in Cutler Ridge.

ROBERT DUYOS

cle, but the military force, which would grow to nearly 20,000, was at once creative and multi-talented.

Faced with a communications dilemma — people didn't know where to get help because they had no electricity or telephone service — the military gave out 10,000 radios with batteries.

Unable to make a massive chow call to their 20 scattered mobile kitchens, the signal corps lofted giant helium balloons over each site to mark the way.

Hamstrung by massive traffic jams, the air corps simply moved crucial supplies by helicopter.

The military feeder lines began delivering by ship and by air: eight 750-kw generators, three mobile hospitals, 55 helicopters, 1,500 vehicles.

It became the largest U.S. military rescue mission in history. And the clock had just begun on how long they would stay.

"We will do whatever it takes for as long as it takes to put the lives of these people back on solid ground," promised Col. Alex Sullivan, commander of the first wave of federal troops.

But unlike a typical military operation, the troops had to deal with civilians who weren't used to lining up on command or recognizing who was in charge.

"When we first arrived, a lot of the civilian problem was that no one knew who was in charge," said Col. Steve Ritter. "In the military, there is always someone in charge."

The line of command led to Lt. Gen. Samuel Ebbesen, once chief of staff for Gen. Norman Schwarzkopf.

But this was a different war than Schwarzkopf ran in Operation Desert Storm. The enemy was a chameleon, changing from thirst to disease, from hunger to shelter, from shock to frustration.

So, too, the army's defense changed. Instead of satellites and smart bombs, they used order and compassion.

Men dressed in war-like fatigues shuffled boxes of diapers. A lieutenant colonel tipped fresh water to the thirsty lips of an elderly woman. Children followed uniformed soldiers around like they were the pied pipers of an eerie new hamlet.

American troops reached out to take the hands of Americans like themselves.

It was a first-hand lesson in the New World order.

"You don't ever get to see the military help you directly," commented David Jones, a newly homeless Florida City resident who was one of the first to greet the troops. "You just hear about them fighting in places. This is what they ought to do."

— JONATHON KING

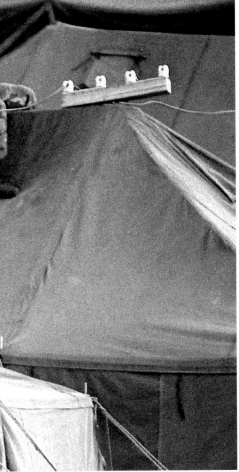

SUSAN G. STOCKER

Above: Two Marines rest on top of tents being set up for hurricane refugees at Harris Field. The Marines were connecting power lines to the tent city.

Right: Spc. Michael Cleary gives a bag of ice to a boy who was overlooked in a Homestead ice line.

URSULA E. SEEMANN

Lt. Col. John Hering takes care of Jason DeLeon, who fell and cut his head. Sgt. Patricia Dawson-Gayle holds Christian DeLeon.

JOE RAEDLE

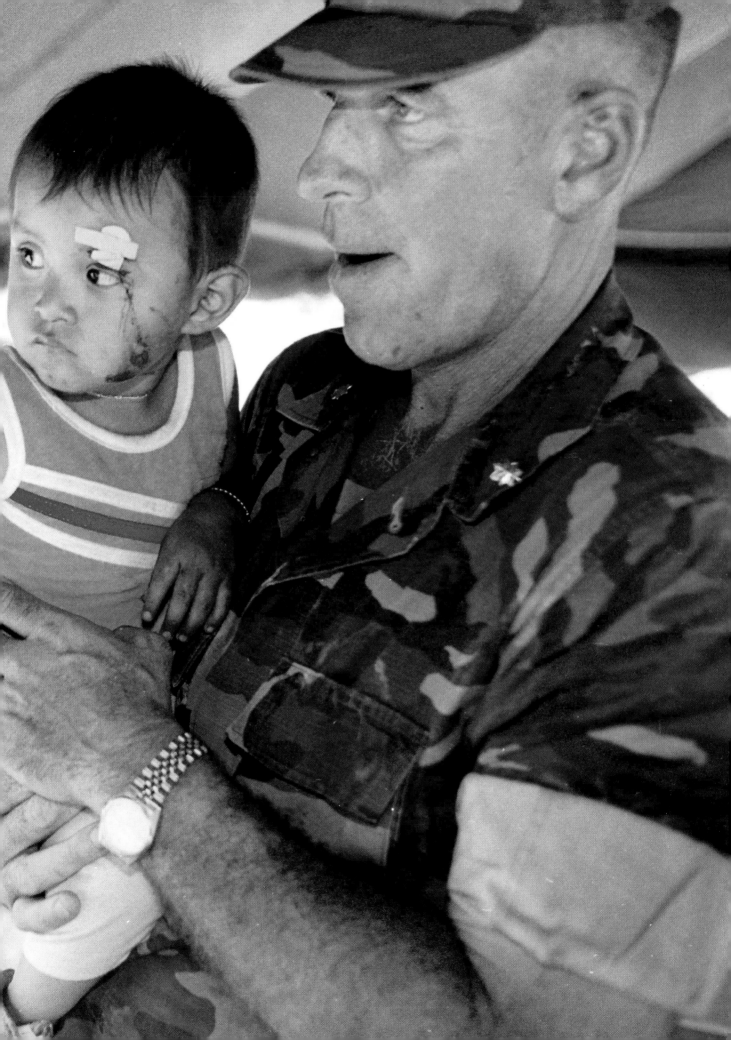

LOU TOMAN

Jay Martin wheels plywood into his truck as Donald Jarvi ties plywood to his car roof in the parking lot of Builders Square on Sheridan Street, Hollywood.

'We Were Very Lucky'

In Fort Lauderdale, the storm began inside a Winn-Dixie grocery store.

Nervous shoppers bumped carts jammed with plastic jugs of water, batteries, candles and anything edible in a can.

"It's getting worse and worse and worse," fretted cashier Gail Hollingsworth.

It was getting worse all over Broward County. At gas stations, at pharmacies, at lumber yards. By early Saturday evening, a Home Depot in Davie sold 3,300 sheets of plywood and promised another 7,500 for delivery the next day.

This wasn't panic, exactly. But it was a healthy fear, and by Sunday it was palpable.

Northbound turnpike traffic backed up from Lantana to Sunrise. An armada of boats streamed along the New River, searching for safe harbor.

As many as 50 people queued up at ATM machines. "You don't even know if there will be any money left when you get up there," said Larry Sherman, 30th in a Coral Springs cash-line.

Thousands of residents evacuated coastal areas, converting canyons of high-rise condos into ghost towns. Some 22,000 Broward evacuees huddled in shelters. And at least 1,500 pregnant women raced to hospitals.

Some just prayed.

"It is in the hands of God," said one of the faithful at Saint Ambrose Catholic Church. "Only God knows what will happen."

As late as Sunday night, the National Hurricane Center still predicted Andrew would storm ashore in Dade County — or Broward.

"We sat there holding our breath," says Arthur St. Amand, Broward's emergency chief. "We were sitting there going, 'Is it going to hit Fort Lauderdale? Is it going south?'"

The hurricane's massive arms crashed across south Dade County early Monday morning, but its fingertips slapped Broward.

Wind gusts, clocked as high as 105 mph, batted down anything weakly rooted. The roof of the beachside Bahama Hotel ripped off. Mobile homes smashed. A

High winds and tides uprooted this Fort Lauderdale Beach sign, carrying it 100 feet across A1A.

MICHAEL MALONE

WELCOME TO
FORT LAUDERDALE
BEACH

two-block stretch of unfinished oceanfront wall toppled.

Hundreds of trees and power lines were pushed over and electricity for more than 400,000 homes and businesses was knocked out. Few traffic lights worked. Sand was piled a foot deep on State Road A1A.

Andrew also displayed a sick sense of humor. The plywood covering the front windows of Angel Barracco's Sunrise home were scrawled with a dare in brown paint: "We're waiting for you, Andrew. Go ahead, try me."

The hurricane passed up the boarded house — but tossed a tree onto Barracco's '82 Camaro.

And for Mark Herndon and Brett Knesz, the post-Andrew fishing was great. Not off Hollywood beach, but on it.

They scooped up red snapper and grouper that had been hurled into a gully by the waves. "We got about 100 pounds," Herndon said. "Good eating."

In the hours just before, during and after the hurricane, many of the mothers-in-waiting had their babies — making naming the newborns easy. Andrew Michael Simone, Andrea Hopkins and Kyle Hurricane Harmyk were among at least 22 babies born in Broward hospitals by noon Monday.

Broward was one of three counties declared federal disaster areas by President Bush. But as word of Dade's ravages slowly filtered out, many north of the disaster zones repeated the same four-word mantra: "We were very lucky."

Relief efforts quickly cranked into gear. Thankful residents donated bottled water, canned food, clothes, money. And time.

Desperate Dade residents streamed like Third World refugees into Broward, seeking something to eat, something to drink, someplace to sleep.

And the scope of the tragedy

just a one-hour drive south of Broward sank in. Flickering television images raised the specter of what might have been.

"I was watching it last night on TV and I started to cry," said one Broward woman. "Some of those people have worked all their lives to have what they have and in an hour it's all destroyed.

"You don't know who the unfortunate ones are going to be," she mused. "We were very lucky."

— *BOB KNOTTS*

A toppled houseboat was among the damage at Marina Bay Resort, just north of State Road 84 and west of Interstate 95.

ROBERT DUY

Kurt Mickle of Budget Tree Services cleans up seagrape trees outside Fountainhead Condominiums on Ocean Drive in Lauderdale-by-the-Sea.

TIM RIVERS

JILL GUTTMAN

Alvena Carney, 89, of Gulf Stream, spends the night in Atlantic High School gym.

The Fortunate Pitch In

They wiped store shelves clean, boarded up their homes and slept fitfully Sunday night.

Come Monday, Palm Beach County awoke to greet the gray dawn with a collective sigh of relief.

Yes, there were trees down. And, for some, power and telephones were dead.

But they were alive. With their homes intact. The storm had threatened. But Palm Beach County beat the odds.

Then came a second dawning as Palm Beach County realized its good fortune had come at Dade County's tragic expense.

The sighs of relief became gasps of disbelief as residents saw ghastly TV images revealing the storm's devastation less than a hundred miles to the south.

Then, in what would become the county's biggest outpouring of help, residents mobilized to ease the suffering in Dade.

"You can't just sit down in front of the television," recalls Dr. Lawrence Grayhills, who gathered medical supplies to take to the hurricane-ravaged area. "You have to get off your butt and do something."

Everywhere, people helped:

• Small-business folk like surveyor Jeff Stark in Boynton Beach, who tacked signs on his buildings asking for donations and rented trucks to transport goods.

• Housewives, like Sandy Phipps, of Boca Raton, who organized a food drive at Addison Mizner Elementary, then persuaded Sears to donate trash cans to hold the goods.

• Thousands of residents with specialized skills — from con-

voys of construction workers to doctors and nurses from St. Mary's Hospital who rode south on buses to help their weary counterparts.

• And everywhere, boxes seeking donations of clothing, canned food and money.

But, there was a growing realization that this huge outpouring of care had to be organized.

So the Exposition Centre at the South Florida Fairgrounds became a giant food distribution and command post.

Overnight, the usual site of rock concerts and livestock exhibits swarmed with hundreds of volunteers.

"I don't want to be guilty of doing nothing," says Leo Kaufman, 80, of West Palm Beach. "God helped us up here so we've got to help them."

— *JANE MUSGRAVE*

MARK RANDALL

Above: Volunteers sort and pack food donations at a Red Cross clearinghouse at the South Florida Fairgrounds.

Left: Gerald Newton of Boynton Beach scuttled his boat to prevent storm surge from tossing it into the pilings.

MARK RANDALL

JILL GUTTMAN

Joseph Baine, 55, of the Bahamas, grieves for his daughter Yvonne, who drowned in the hurricane. "She stayed here to be close to me. Now she gone."

The First Blow

Andrew slammed into the Bahama Islands around 2:30 Sunday afternoon, some 14 hours before it struck South Florida.

Few residents of this 700-island nation were prepared. The last major hurricane to hit the Bahamas was Hurricane David in 1979, a mild storm that destroyed a few buildings and flooded streets.

But Andrew proved different — and deadly.

When the skies cleared Monday morning, four Bahamians lay dead and 5,000 were homeless, victims of a towering storm surge and winds of more than 150 miles an hour.

Ploughing westward through the less populated center of the island chain, Andrew spared the Bahamas' major centers of population in Freeport and Nassau.

Hardest hit was a cluster of islands called North Eleuthera, its pastel homes, quaint hotels and tiny fishing boats obliterated by an 18-foot wall of water and Andrew's devastating winds.

Stunned government officials say property damages will be "in the tens of millions."

Picking through the wreckage of his home the morning after the storm, Joseph Baine mourned his daughter Yvonne Cash, a 37-year-old mother of seven who drowned.

"She stayed here to be close to me," Baine sighs, scratching his white whiskers. "Now she gone."

On Current Island, a tidal wave left only one house standing and 125 people homeless.

Monica Algreen remembers trying to hide behind the door of her Current Island house as the wave hit it.

She ran into one bedroom but the water rushed in after her. Unable to swim, she and her husband, Cloide, climbed atop their mattress and floated up to the ceiling where they prayed until the wind and water receded.

"It's a miracle we did not die. We don't know how we survived," Algreen says.

— *GARRY PIERRE-PIERRE*

STEVE LASKY/THE TIMES-PICAYUNE

Janet Hansche and her family in New Orleans were prepared for the worst. Her son used a vacuum cleaner to inflate their rubber dinghy — just in case.

Fear in Cajun Country

The picture from Florida was worth just three words: Get out now!

In southern Louisiana on the morning of Tuesday, Aug. 25, the newspaper photo of what Hurricane Andrew had done one day earlier to Homestead was all people needed to see.

They nailed plywood to their doors and criss-crossed tape on the windows like giant asterisks.

Then they fled.

By Tuesday evening, Houma, Morgan City, Franklin, New Iberia — cities strung like pearls through Cajun country between New Orleans and Lafayette — were boarded up and deserted.

Traffic backed up 25 miles with cars headed north, away from the storm.

The sky darkened. The first drops of rain began to spatter on the empty streets.

The bayou country is veined with rivers and levees. Swamps rise green and algae-covered nearly to the level of the roads.

In Morgan City, the municipal auditorium brimmed with 1,000 refugees. Legs, blankets, mattresses, children and potato chips were tangled on the hard floor.

The full force of Hurricane Andrew slammed into Franklin, a small, wood-sided Cajun town of about 10,000, shortly after midnight. Between 1 and 3:30, the wind gauge on the courthouse never dipped below 140 miles per hour — and sometimes it read as high as 168.

Then it snapped off.

David Naquin, chief detective of the St. Mary's Parish Sheriff's Department, was holed up in the courthouse. Andrew stalled twice, he said, once before the eye passed over, and once after. Its winds clawed at the town for 11 hours.

Naquin had been through hurricanes before. But not like this.

"I've never had one sit on top of me for hours and hours and hours the way this one did," he said.

Jennifer Naquin cowered in her home. "You could feel the house rumbling like it was going to pick up and go," she said.

David Rose was in his gas station. "I laid on the floor last night and prayed," he said. "I said, 'If you're ready for me, I'm here.'"

Clutching family photos, Kelly Forsythe searches through the remains of her family's house in Reserve, La.

G. ANDREW BOYD/
THE TIMES-PICAYUNE

Kevin Siguie looks at a trophy found in the remains of his father's business near New Iberia, La.

The storm roared through Baldwin and Jeanerette and New Iberia, toppling trees, tossing trailers in the air like toys, ripping roofs clean away.

The streets were eerie on Wednesday morning. It was gray, rainy and windy; the back side of the terrible storm had not yet departed. But in the misty light, the damage could be seen.

Not a building in Franklin escaped damaged.

All along U.S. 90, walls were torn from houses and stores. Power lines were down. Trees blocked streets.

The state's precious sugar cane was wrecked. Field after field, hundreds and hundreds of acres, ruined. The green stalks stayed bent to the ground, all in the same direction, as if the hurricane were still blowing.

The storm claimed nine lives in Louisiana.

In Baldwin, Mark Firmin found his trailer overturned, squashed and split open like a rotten tomato. He crawled in to try to retrieve a few belongings.

His wife and daughter were upstate. Secely, almost 4, had not wanted to leave — she liked their home, she told her daddy, and she was afraid for it.

Firmin had talked to his family on the phone. But he had not found the words to tell Secely their home was destroyed.

"It hurts, man, it hurts," he said, his eyes reddening.

The next day was sunny, a sweet, warm, Louisiana summer day. Traffic backed up along U.S. 90, southbound this time, as people streamed back into the area, ignoring the pleas of officials who wanted them to stay away because there was no power or food.

There was a burst of euphoria: They had survived. The flooding had not been bad.

Relief organizations began cooking meals for the hungry.

People happily set about the business of clearing their driveways and fixing their homes and repairing their roofs.

"How'd you make out?" they called to each other from rooftops.

"We made out OK," would come the response.

— *DON MELVIN*

SEAN DOUGHERTY

A postcard shows what this part of Fairchild Tropical Garden in south Dade looked like before Andrew. The landscape will take decades to restore.

An Alien Landscape

After Andrew, it's much easier to get lost.

"It's hard to tell where you really are," says Allison Straight, who lived in south Dade until her home was smashed.

Andrew turned yesterday's familiar world into an alien landscape — destroying Metrozoo and the Monkey Jungle, leveling the verdant state park on Key Biscayne, wasting Fairchild Tropical Garden, even crushing a once-splendid cottage in Vizcaya, the fabled Deering Estate.

Coconut Grove is hardly a grove anymore, so many trees are gone. Besides wind damage, a wall of water fell on the "in" spot beside the bay, flooding homes and turning foliage brown.

Then there was Andrew's salt-

> **'The first day, I didn't cry until I left. You can't cry while you're there; you won't get any work done.'**
>
> KAREN MACIAG
> Metrozoo volunteer

water rain, a potential slow killer for South Florida's subtropical landscape. Months from now, salt poisoning from Andrew's ocean-scooped rains could cause plants to turn black and die. This is David Alexander's fear.

"My personal estimate is two to three years before we get green canopies like we had before," says Alexander, of the Coconut

Grove Local Development Corp.

Hardest hit was Metrozoo, where tornadoes ripped through acres of trees.

Netting crashed down on an exhibit of 335 exotic birds, destroying it. The monorail blew off its tracks. The second floor of the restaurant disappeared.

After the storm, workers scrambled over fallen trees, steel girders and overturned vehicles to reach the animals. Blunt trauma killed some: an ostrich, a wild Asian donkey, two antelope-like mammals and countless birds. A missing baby gibbon was presumed dead.

Four days later, the alien landscape almost caused volunteer Karen Maciag to miss the turn into Metrozoo.

Above: Lush foliage lined the path to Vizcaya's entrance until Andrew blew in.
SEAN DOUGHERTY

Left: The hurricane flattened trees at Bill Baggs State Park, at the southern tip of Key Biscayne.
CARL SEIBERT

"The first day, I didn't cry until I left," says Maciag. "You can't cry while you're there; you won't get any work done."

Some Dade officials fear staggering reconstruction costs will prevent the zoo from reopening — a dire forecast zoo employees steadfastly refuse to believe.

It's a matter of spirit, the zoo workers say, pointing to people like John "Action" Jackson, a private pilot who flew mercy missions of food into the zoo after the storm.

On one trip, zoo spokesman Ron Magill watched in horror as Jackson's plane crashed in the zoo's parking lot.

Magill ran over as Jackson emerged from the wreckage.

"Damn!" said the pilot, as Magill recalls. "I'm just so ticked off about this plane. Now I have to find a trailer."

In the days following Andrew, workers shipped most of the park's exotic animals off to temporary homes in other zoos around the country.

At Fairchild Tropical Garden, a small army of volunteers was formed to clear debris and save delicate foliage from insects, fungus and South Florida's searing summer heat.

Fairchild is the only tropical botanical garden in the contiguous United States. Before Hurricane Andrew, it had the largest collection of palms and cycads in the world.

"It turned the landscape back 50 to 100 years," says director William Klein Jr.

Andrew's winds toppled jungle groves, turning the garden's rainforest into twisted piles of sticks. The roof on the rare plant house collapsed. Inside, what was once a precisely arranged paradise now looks like someone's forgotten garden, random and unkempt.

But here, too, there is hope.

A roof beam missed crushing a rare cycad — one of only four collected in the world — by a mere six inches. And the botanists have plenty of room for planting new specimens.

Where others would see devastation, Klein sees a chance to garden.

"This is to us the story of tending nature," he says. "That's what is missing from the world."

— *KAREN SAMPLES*

A member of the Florida National Guard patrols the Coral Castle tourist attraction in south Dade. Foliage was severely damaged; the castle fared much better.

SUSAN G. STOCKER

Left: Volunteers help clear debris from the rainforest exhibit at Fairchild Tropical Garden.

SEAN DOUGHERTY

Far left: The Weeks Air Museum at Tamiami Airport was destroyed.

CARL SEIBERT

URSULA E. SEEMANN

Two days after Andrew, the 18th hole at Sabal Palm Golf Course in Tamarac still was playable. However, sobering reminders remained.

Playing for Keeps

The morning after Hurricane Andrew, University of Miami coach Dennis Erickson waded through knee-deep water to his Coral Reef home.

Anxious questions plagued his every step.

Was the house intact?

Was the family dog alive?

And what of his players?

"It sure kind of put everything into perspective," said Erickson, who lasted out the hurricane with his family at an assistant's house.

Perspective. Erickson and four UM assistants lost their homes.

Perspective. The Miami Dolphins, with a home opener against New England scheduled for 13 days after Andrew, moved the game to an open date six weeks later. At Joe Robbie Stadium, they collected food,

pumped out 9,000 pounds of ice daily, and became a staging area for law enforcement and emergency officials.

Perspective. The UM football team moved practices 142 miles from Coral Gables to Vero Beach, where there was water, food and electricity, but no mental relief from the horrors left behind. Senior linebacker Micheal Barrow arrived a week later. He was helping his mother stitch her life together after her home was destroyed.

Overnight, some of South Florida's famous names became foot soldiers in the volunteer relief army. Dolphins linebacker John Offerdahl and 15 employees of his Broward bagel shops cooked and delivered 6,000 bagels to south Dade.

Jennifer Capriati donated half

her U.S. Open winnings to Red Cross relief efforts. Andre Dawson skipped two Chicago Cubs games to return home and help family members whose homes were destroyed. Four Miami Heat players and general partner Lewis Schaffel rode two helicopters to south Dade to help relief efforts and Dolphins players delivered and unloaded a supply truck.

The morning after Andrew, the Ericksons began cleaning roof from their carpet and mud from their walls. The sole good news was that their golden retriever survived. He evidently ran out the garage door when it was smashed open and lasted out the storm until a neighbor saw him and brought him inside.

The dog's name: Champ.

— DAVE HYDE

CARL SEIBERT

Flipped cars cover rubble inside the garage of a home. Reconstruction is expected to add 5,000 to 7,000 home-building jobs in Dade County.

Can We Rebuild?

Shrimper John McNulty and his family survived Hurricane Andrew, but his houseboat and job didn't.

They faced the future with three dogs, some clothes and a 1975 pickup truck with a hole in the radiator.

"The only job in my entire life I liked is shrimping," he said. "Now what?"

Hurricane Andrew cost thousands of Floridians their jobs as well as their homes.

Out of destruction comes growth, yet within two weeks of the storm, it was too soon to say if the hurricane would be a loss or gain for South Florida's economy.

Homestead Air Force Base and 8,700 related jobs might be gone forever. President Bush promised that the base would be rebuilt; if it isn't, expect a $400 million hit to the economy.

Dade County's $1 billion agriculture industry was leveled. The hurricane smashed crops, equipment and buildings, idling more than 20,000 workers.

"The sad part is, our farmers should be planting ... but they have no equipment," said Shirey Sickle. "Even if they could plant the beans, the potatoes, the squash, there's no packing house to send it to."

Small business was decimated. About 90 percent of the 2,100 businesses in the Homestead and South Dade chambers of commerce were smashed. Firms faced months of rebuilding; many wouldn't be back.

Big retailers like Bloomingdale's, Mervyn's, Levitz Furniture, Home Depot, Winn-Dixie and Publix all lost stores. The Cutler Ridge Mall was destroyed.

The storm did $100 million worth of damage to Florida Power & Light Co.'s Turkey Point nuclear power plant, damaging one smokestack so badly it had to be demolished.

But there was good news.

Insurance would ease the blow. Insurors expected $7.3 billion in claims, making Andrew the costliest natural disaster in history.

Dade County's Beacon Council was seeking $15 million in emergency state loans. Federal Small Business Administration loans were to be available.

Retailers in northern Dade, Broward and Palm Beach counties benefited from the hurricane: They were swamped as vic-

Above: A member of the Florida National Guard stands watch for looters outside the heavily damaged Bloomingdale's store at The Falls shopping center in Kendall.
SUSAN G. STOCKER

Right: A weakened smokestack is demolished at Florida Power & Light's generating plant at Turkey Point, where damage was estimated at $100 million.
JUDY SLOAN REICH

Far right: Andrew peeled the roof off a Holsum bread distribution center and scattered delivery trucks parked outside.
CARL SEIBERT

LOU TOMAN

A plant farm near Homestead lies in ruin. Hurricane damage idled more than 20,000 agricultural workers.

tims sought food, water, medical and building supplies.

Hotels and restaurants were full of rescue workers, insurance adjusters and homeless residents.

And the construction and repair industries were expected to boom. From 5,000 to 7,000 new construction jobs were expected in Dade County.

"The recession — make that depression — is over," said West Palm Beach contractor David Graves.

To rebuild, people would have insurance checks and Federal Housing Administration disaster loans. Banks promised streamlined loans.

The marine industry was expected to revive from a deep slump; the storm damaged thousands of boats in Dade.

Tourism, an $11 billion industry, was relatively unscathed as far as buildings and attractions.

Some Dade attractions like Vizcaya were moderately damaged, and Metrozoo was devastated. However, major hotels, cruise ships and ports escaped intact.

Image may be another matter. Andrew had barely left Florida for Louisiana when the Division of Tourism put a $47,000 ad in *USA Today*: "Florida, we're still open."

"Most people have very short memories. We're all sort of banking on that," said Donal Dermody, director of the Nova University Center for Hospitality Management.

But you don't have to be a tourist to be scared of hurricanes.

"People are going to think about moving out of here because it's known as a hurricane zone," said retail consultant William Wholey.

Within days, however, Andrew had boosted the sagging real estate market. Homes and warehouses were headed for 100 percent rental. A soft market had been turned into a "Manhattan for housing," one real estate agent said.

Michael Cannon, president of Appraisal and Real Estate Economics Associates, has seen five hurricanes since 1948; each boosted the economy.

"People now say, 'I'm getting out of here,'" he said. "A year or two from now, people will forget about it."

— *DAVID ALTANER*

Homestead Air Force Base, all but destroyed, provides 8,700 jobs and adds $400 million each year to Dade County's economy.

JOHN CURRY

CONSTRUCTION

WARREN RICHEY

The $400,000 Cutler Ridge home of the Michael McCaffrey family was destroyed, while a next-door neighbor's home suffered minor damage.

Unsafe in a Storm

In the face of nature's fury, man's creations stand little chance.

As it sheared the flatlands of south Dade, Andrew made this distressingly clear. Our homes, our fortresses, crumpled beneath the storm's pure energy.

But just as much, they fell due to the hands of the people who built them, people who cut corners and used cheap materials and then skimped on even those, people who slapped houses together, painted them pretty, and then just walked away.

When Dr. Wen Chang wondered why some houses survived while others were blown to bits, it didn't take long to find answers as he toured south Dade's storm-ravaged suburbs.

Chang, professor emeritus at the University of Miami school of engineering, believes some builders flat-out lie about the integrity of their homes. And the

> **'This either was incompetence or mass corruption. When people buy a home, they assume that the [inspection] people do their job.'**
>
> E. CLAY SHAW
> U.S. representative, R-Fort Lauderdale

inspectors who are supposed to make sure new homes meet code aren't doing the job.

Consider the fates of two houses standing side-by-side on Southwest 86th Court in Cutler Ridge.

Richard Wiskeman's house was scuffed a bit when a piece of plywood from a neighbor's home smashed through the sliding glass doors. The wind roared through the gap, blowing out two

windows up front. But that was it.

Wiskeman's neighbors barely escaped with their lives. Michael McCaffrey, his wife and two young children huddled in a small bathroom as Andrew ripped away the roof of their $400,000 home. They fled to a closet until that section of roof came apart and then crowded into their car in the garage until the winds subsided.

Chang poked through the wreckage of the roof, pulling out chunks of wood that he labeled an inferior grade. One piece from a truss was so badly knotted that the wood had broken clean through.

The bottom line: Price is no guarantee that your home is well-built. Neither is appearance.

Neighbors work together in a home ripped open by the hurricane.

JOE RAEDLE

Above: Two Cutler Ridge residents comfort each other within hours after Andrew stripped their home of much of its roof and walls.
Right: This concrete-block home in Perrine was blown to bits in the hurricane, but the bathtub remained in place, with the water running.

SEAN DOUGHERTY

A look inside damaged homes

Shoddy construction and inadequate building inspection came to the fore in the wake of Hurricane Andrew. Here are examples of dangers that are hidden once construction is completed.

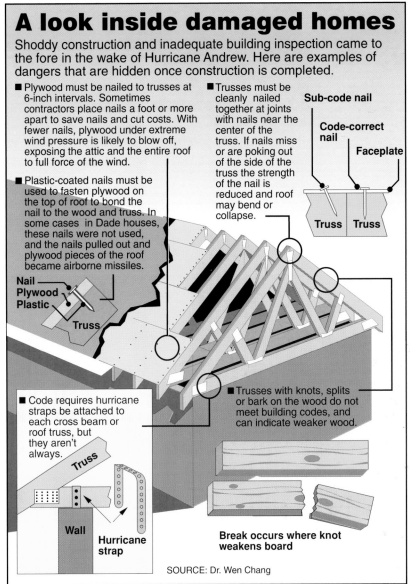

■ Plywood must be nailed to trusses at 6-inch intervals. Sometimes contractors place nails a foot or more apart to save nails and cut costs. With fewer nails, plywood under extreme wind pressure is likely to blow off, exposing the attic and the entire roof to full force of the wind.

■ Plastic-coated nails must be used to fasten plywood on the top of roof to bond the nail to the wood and truss. In some cases in Dade houses, these nails were not used, and the nails pulled out and plywood pieces of the roof became airborne missiles.

Nail
Plywood
Plastic
Truss

■ Trusses must be cleanly nailed together at joints with nails near the center of the truss. If nails miss or are poking out of the side of the truss the strength of the nail is reduced and roof may bend or collapse.

Sub-code nail
Code-correct nail
Faceplate
Truss   Truss

■ Trusses with knots, splits or bark on the wood do not meet building codes, and can indicate weaker wood.

■ Code requires hurricane straps be attached to each cross beam or roof truss, but they aren't always.

Truss
Wall
Hurricane strap

Break occurs where knot weakens board

SOURCE: Dr. Wen Chang

ANDY DORSETT

If the builder and the inspectors haven't done their jobs, you're in trouble.

Outside, Chang says, a home can seem rock solid. But its unseen structure can be "a piece of junk."

Sadly, no one in the construction trade seems that surprised by Chang's findings.

In 1990, a Dade County grand jury found that inspectors falsified work sheets, never bothered to climb on roofs they certified, and were prone to political pressure to go easy on certain builders.

Three years earlier, 24 Dade builders were arrested for trying to bribe an undercover cop they thought was a building inspector.

In Broward, inspectors fail to catch code violations in up to 20 percent of the reviews they perform in some months, though the usual average is lower, about 5 percent.

It took a storm like Andrew to show us how deadly this can be.

"This either was incompetence or mass corruption," fumed U.S. Rep. E. Clay Shaw of Fort Lauderdale. "When people buy a home, they assume that the [inspection] people do their job. For people to be put in an unsafe structure, that is unforgivable."

— *WARREN RICHEY,*
FRED SCHULTE AND
MICHAEL E. YOUNG

JIM VIRGA

Shoppers scrambling for hurricane provisions pack an Albertsons store in Delray Beach on the afternoon before Andrew struck.

They'll Just Get Out

We lived with the same old warnings for years: Come hurricane season, prepare for the worst.

The instructions were everywhere, on television and radio, stuck inside special sections of the newspaper — even printed on the sides of grocery bags.

Trouble was, no one knew what it meant to prepare for the worst.

Killer storms were the stuff of history books.

And then came Andrew.

"We knew we were getting a hurricane," says Jim Jacks from under the gutted roof of his Perrine home. "We did not know it would be this bad."

Jacks nailed plywood over his windows the day before Andrew. His wife filled pots and pans with water. They had batteries, flashlights, a portable radio and canned goods.

Their careful planning did little good against Andrew's 140 mph

> **'We knew we were getting a hurricane. We did not know it would be this bad.'**
>
> JIM JACKS
> Perrine resident

winds. The storm ripped the plywood from the windows and tore off the roof. Rain poured in to wreck the batteries.

Next time, it will be different, Jacks vows.

"I hear it's a hurricane, and I'll get out."

South Florida had plenty of time to prepare for Andrew. The National Hurricane Center kept us informed of the storm's path and destructive nature.

Officials say the evacuation of the coast went smoothly. But many remained in evacuation areas, including thousands in

high-rise apartments along the coast in Broward and north Dade counties.

"The one thing I hope is that people in Broward County realize how lucky they are and don't go around bragging that they have been through a hurricane," says Arthur St. Amand, director of Broward's Emergency Preparedness Division. "Believe me, they have not."

For many of those hardest hit in Dade, the best of preparations did little good.

While Ken Brook failed to board up his home, his neighbor's home is storm-shattered proof of how inadequate covered windows could be against Andrew's strongest winds.

"He did everything according to the book and his damage is astronomical," Brook says. "He had sandbags — sandbags!"

Andrew's devastation showed how even our best laid post-storm

What if...

Destruction would have been much worse if Andrew had come ashore farther north, in one of South Florida's more densely populated areas. This shows who and what was at risk if Andrew's 10- to 12-mile eye made landfall near Fort Lauderdale's Las Olas Boulevard **(A)** or in central Boca Raton **(B)**.

...it hit Fort Lauderdale

People at risk

Population: 614,558

Pop. in group quarters (nursing homes, dorms, jail, shelters, etc.): 9,338

Age 17 and under: 128,710

Age 18 to 64: 369,861

Age 65 and up: 115,987

Homes at risk

Value of owner-occupied one-family homes: **$12.6 billion**

Value of rent paid (except one-family homes): **$42.5 million**

Total all homes: 302,003

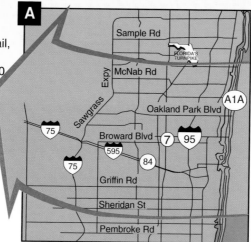

...it hit Boca Raton

People at risk

Population: 320,861

Pop. in group quarters (nursing homes, dorms, jail, shelters, etc.): 3,944

Age 17 and under: 56,450

Age 18 to 64: 177,028

Age 65 and up: 87,383

Homes at risk

Value of owner-occupied one-family homes: **$10.23 billion**

Value of rent paid (except one-family homes): **$21.5 million**

Total all homes: 179,304

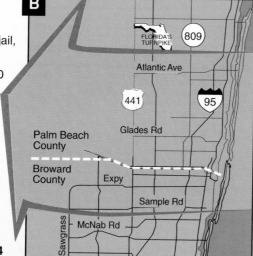

Andrew's actual path

Dade: South of SW 152nd Street

Population: 202,036

Value of owner-occupied one-family homes: **$3.1 billion**

Value of rent paid (except one-family homes): **$8.3 million**

Total all homes: 71,436

SOURCE: *Sun-Sentinel* analysis of 1990 U.S. Census data   Staff research/SCOTT ANDERSON

AARON E. PORTER

PREPARATION HINTS

South Floridians had become dangerously complacent about preparing early for a hurricane. Andrew may have forever changed that. Some hints on how to get ready before every hurricane season starts:

START OF THE SEASON

• Start planning and preparing immediately.

• Gather supplies to avoid last-minute rushes on hardware stores and markets.

• Learn the elevation of your area and the flooding and storm surge history.

• Learn the location of shelters and evacuation routes.

• If you own a boat, determine where to move it.

• Check your insurance to be sure you have the coverage you want and need.

• Maintain an up-to-date inventory of your possessions to assist in settling insurance claims if your home is damaged. Include a description of each item, serial number, the date of purchase and price. Keep in a safe-deposit box.

SUPPLY LIST

• Essential medicines; extra prescriptions.

• First-aid kit.

• Fire extinguisher (ABC type).

• Battery-operated radio with extra batteries.

• Flashlight with extra batteries and bulbs.

• Lantern and fuel.

• Sleeping bags and blankets.

• Enough water for a week (two quarts a person a day in clean glass or plastic containers). Bleach or tablets for purifying water.

• Enough nonperishable food for two weeks.

• Baby food, diapers and formula.

• Cooler and ice or dry ice.

• Emergency cooking equipment, such as canned heat, charcoal for grill or propane for gas grill. (Gas and charcoal grills must not be used indoors.)

• Matches (kept in waterproof container).

• Paper plates, cups, napkins and paper towels. Plastic utensils.

• Manual can opener.

• Toiletries.

Angel Barraco of Sunrise left a message for Andrew during his preparations; Andrew answered with a fury.

plans can be blown away: It's one thing to collect goods and food for thousands of storm victims, but a logistical nightmare getting them to those in need.

Bureaucratic delays proved infuriating — just as they were in South Carolina after Hugo in 1989. Andrew again made clear the need for one agency with muscle to serve as a clearinghouse for information and action.

As Charleston, S.C., Mayor Joseph P. Riley Jr. told Congress, federal disaster relief should be directed by someone in the army "who hates paperwork."

Federal officials during Hugo asked Riley for an assessment of need before a generator was purchased. Riley was flabbergasted.

"I said, 'Assessment! There is no power for 80 miles!'"

Along with more than 60,000 homes, Andrew obliterated any notion that life-saving help is always a phone call away.

Andrew's ultimate lesson: Sometimes the best thing to do is run.

"I would get out," says Camille Geraldi. "I would never, ever, ever stay in a hurricane again. It was the most devastating thing to be that scared, and then to open the door and see what it had done.

"I wouldn't even go upstate. I'd get in a plane and get out of here," Geraldi says.

"It doesn't matter how prepared you are when that thing comes blowing through your house."

— *TREVOR JENSEN*

Northbound cars jam Florida's Turnpike at the Cypress Creek toll plaza as evacuees flee South Florida the afternoon before Andrew came ashore.

CARL SEIBERT

SUN-SENTINEL FILE PHOTO

A car off Federal Highway in Fort Lauderdale after Hurricane Betsy in 1965.

Lessons of a Lifetime

No question, the old man says. No question at all, but there is a pattern to things.

Pelicans on the wing know to skim across the water in a perfect "V."

Babies know how to breathe straight from the womb.

And hurricanes, says this leather-skinned man who's spent a lifetime fishing the Keys, know when to come to Florida.

"Stone crabs and lobster thin out and it takes a bad storm to churn things up," Jimmy Woods says. "Few months later your traps'll be full."

Jimmy has seen his share of hurricanes while fishing the Keys.

Been so many, he disremembers their actual number.

But at 77, he's survived his deadly share.

He was a boy of 11 when a no-name killer hurricane took more

Jimmy Woods

than 400 lives and leveled most of Miami and Fort Lauderdale back in 1926. Left more than 5,000 people homeless and the real estate boosters sucking wind.

He was 13 when another killer storm struck South Florida in 1928, picking up Lake Okeechobee and turning her loose in western Palm Beach County — with nearly 2,000 souls lost in the flood.

"I heard they were finding bodies for months," he says.

Then came the killer of 1935.

"She hit us with a wall of water 20-foot high and winds that

topped out at more than 250 miles an hour," Jimmy remembers. "She came right through the Florida Keys. Toppled locomotives and passenger cars like they were nothing."

Jimmy was 20 years old when the killer of '35 made him an orphan.

Crushed his mother under an ice box so that it took her more than a week to die. Washed his father into the mangroves where they found the crabs chewing on him several weeks later.

"I was holding on to my baby sister when the water hit," he says. "She was only 18 months old. We went under and the water ripped her out of my arms. Then I came up and something put a three-inch hole in my head."

More than 400 people died.

And now comes Andrew, with 52 dead and more than 250,000

The wreckage of an 11-car passenger train in the Florida Keys on Labor Day in 1935 after an unnamed killer storm.

left homeless.

"Most of her blew by north of us in the Keys," Jimmy says. "Don't think the winds reached more than 55 miles an hour down here in Islamorada. But I think she churned up the bottom so the stone crabs'll be good.

"I feel for those people up there in Dade. I know what they're going through. They was just lucky there was no storm surge like we had," Jimmy says.

"Seems like each generation has to learn about these things. A new crop of people comes along and it takes a storm to teach people they just ain't all that high and mighty. All we got is each other. That's it."

— *JOHN deGROOT*

The bodies of 116 veterans who died in the Sept. 2, 1935, hurricane.

Chronology of a Hurricane

• **AUG. 14** — Begins as a wave of high winds over western Senegal, Africa.

• **AUG. 16** — Declared a tropical depression.

• **AUG. 17** — Becomes Tropical Storm Andrew.

• **AUG. 19** — Loses speed and power, but survives.

• **AUG. 21** — Florida civil defense officials on standby. Key state officials on alert. Red Cross starts preparing shelters.

• **AUG. 22** — Andrew becomes a hurricane early in the morning. Hurricane watch issued from Titusville to the Keys. South Floridians begin to flood stores in search of supplies.

• **AUG. 23** — **8 a.m.** Hurricane warning issued for South Florida. **8:15 a.m.** Evacuation orders begin. Storm shelters open. **2 p.m.** East of the Bahamas, Andrew's sustained winds reach 150 mph. **Mid-afternoon** Traffic jams start choking highways leading north. Evacuations in full force.

7 p.m. Miami Beach is officially closed. **7:30 p.m.** Fort Lauderdale-Hollywood International Airport closes. **8 p.m.** Andrew reaches the Bahamas as a Category 4 hurricane (on a scale of 1 to 5). **9:30 p.m.** Miami International Airport closes.

10 p.m. Andrew leaves the Bahamas with four dead and thousands homeless. **Midnight** Tornado watch in effect in South Florida. Andrew 110 miles east of Miami. Most shelters are filled. Winds pick up. South Florida waits. And prays.

• **AUG. 24** — **12:01 a.m.** Strong winds blast beaches. **3:24 a.m.** Gusts estimated at 140 to 175 mph in Miami. **4 a.m.** Power goes out for most of Broward. **4:55 a.m.** Eye makes landfall in south Dade. Sustained winds about 140 mph. **4:57 a.m.** 164-mph gust at National Hurricane Center. **5:15 a.m.** Eye over Florida City. **6 a.m.** Storm's center tears westward, focused on the Naples area. **6:57 a.m.** Sunrise.

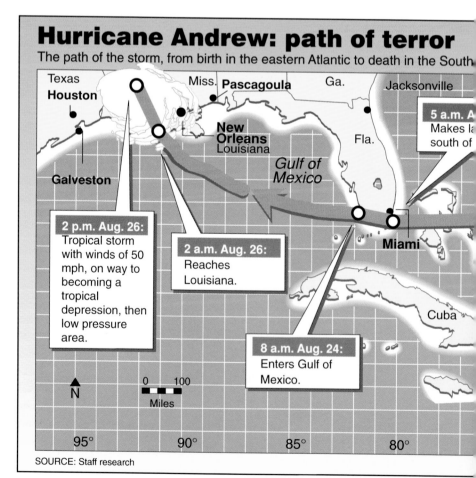

Hurricane Andrew: path of terror

The path of the storm, from birth in the eastern Atlantic to death in the South

Texas
Houston
Miss. **Pascagoula**
Ga.
Jacksonville

New Orleans
Louisiana

Gulf of Mexico

Fla.

5 a.m. A
Makes la
south of

Galveston

2 p.m. Aug. 26:
Tropical storm with winds of 50 mph, on way to becoming a tropical depression, then low pressure area.

2 a.m. Aug. 26:
Reaches Louisiana.

Miami

Cuba

8 a.m. Aug. 24:
Enters Gulf of Mexico.

N

0   100
Miles

95°   90°   85°   80°

SOURCE: Staff research

7:30 a.m. Andrew plows through Marco Island, damages Copeland, Everglades City and Plantation Island. **8 a.m.** Andrew moves into the Gulf of Mexico; winds back to 140 mph.

8:30 a.m. People venture out, tempting remaining squalls. **9 a.m.** Hurricane warnings and watches end for southeast Florida. Damage assessments begin.

10:45 a.m. Governor calls in the National Guard. **Noon** Troops arrive in time to catch looters at Cutler Ridge Mall. Relief efforts get under way. **Midday** Aerial TV footage begins showing first glimpses of the horror in south Dade. Gov. Lawton Chiles, describing

Homestead: "Like an atomic bomb went off."

6 p.m. Air Force One touches down at Opa-locka Airport. President George Bush and Chiles visit the devastated area; Bush designates South Florida a federal disaster area. **7 p.m.** Curfew in effect in Dade.

• **AUG. 25** — Relief efforts and cleanup under way in earnest in Broward and Palm Beach counties. Reports of consumer gouging. Gulf areas prepare for hit. Schools open in Palm Beach County. Power still out to hundreds of thousands. Damage estimate raised to $20 billion.

• **AUG. 26** — **5 a.m.** Southern Louisiana hit. Extreme damage

from New Iberia to Morgan City and Lafayette. **1 p.m.** Downgraded to tropical storm; moves through Mississippi and Alabama. Chaos and misery mount in South Florida; damage and homeless estimates grow; relief efforts are in disarray.

• **AUG. 27** — Plane crashes in south Broward while delivering relief supplies. Cleanup begins in Louisiana. U.S. troops ordered into South Florida, along with mobile kitchens and supplies. Power still out to 389,000 in South Florida. Andrew loses tropical depression status.

Words "We will survive" seen painted on fence in Kendall.

— *PATRICIA HODGE*

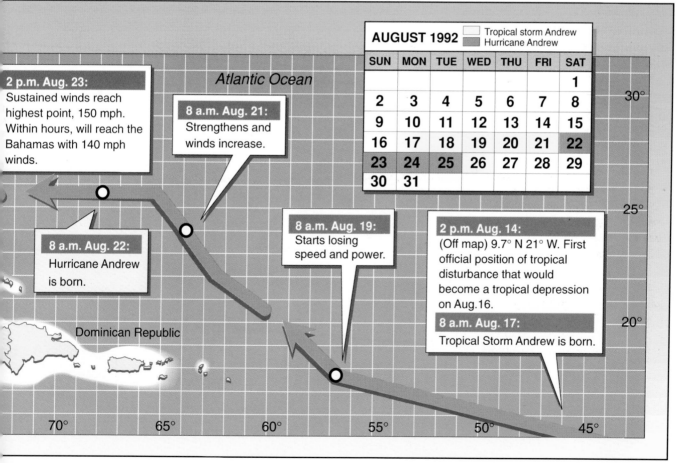

LYNN OCCHIUZZO

A sign of the times in Kendall.

SUSAN G. STOCKER

PHIL SKINNER

Joselyn, 8, brings life to a tent city as mother Olga Barillas watches.

Hope Takes Charge

Amid the debris and devastation in the south Dade neighborhood, a crude drawing stood out.

Taped to a sheet of plywood on the front of one of the homes, the picture showed a lopsided two-story house with one door, one window, a chimney and a tree in front.

It was the typical result of a kindergarten assignment to "draw a picture of your house."

The drawing was not meant to look like the child's house, but to represent the warmth and safety of home.

Scrawled above it in spray paint was the message: "Andrew — Can't Touch This."

Coupled with the drawing, the words spoke volumes. A hurricane can destroy our house, it said, but it can never destroy our home.

It can knock down walls and trees but it can't keep us from putting up new ones. It can interrupt the flow of electricity, but it can never sap our energy.

You may have knocked us down, Andrew, but you can't keep us down.

Only days after Andrew, people who had cowered in fear during the storm and wept after seeing the devastation were beginning to recover their spirit.

Food, water and help arrived. People began to accept and adapt to the new reality, and to realize that all bad things come to an end.

The eerie silence was replaced by the sound of hammering and sawing. Neighbors who had never met shared food, water, tools and strength.

People discovered that, although the fury of such a storm can terrorize us, terror is temporary. The magnitude of the damage it causes can dishearten and discourage us, but it cannot defeat us.

We still have our determination, imagination, intelligence and will to go on.

Most and best of all, we still have each other. Buoyed by the massive relief effort and outpouring of love from people throughout South Florida and the rest of the country, we overcame our initial sense of defeat and began to think of recovery. Slowly but steadily, hope took charge.

With it came the spirit that has characterized every disaster ever suffered and overcome by people of courage. People with gumption and spunk pick themselves up, dust themselves off and start all over again.

The disaster becomes something to read about in history books, but the people rebuild and go on.

That is how it was in Chicago after the fire, Johnstown after the flood, San Francisco after the earthquake and London after the blitz.

And, make no mistake, that is how it will be in South Florida after Andrew.

— *RAY RECCHI*